UNDRESSING *Infidelity*

Why More Wives Are Unfaithful

Their private conversations
with Diane Shader Smith

Published by
Adams Media, an F+W Publications Company
57 Littlefield Street, Avon, MA 02322. U.S.A.
www.adamsmedia.com

ISBN: 1-59337-481-X

Printed in the United States of America.

J I H G F E D C B A

Library of Congress Cataloging-in-Publication Data
Smith, Diane Shader.
Undressing infidelity / Diane Shader Smith.
p.   cm.
ISBN 1-59337-481-X
1. Adultery. 2. Married women—Sexual behavior. I. Title.

HQ806.S56 2005
306.73'6—dc22
                                        2004028172

This publication is designed to provide accurate and authoritative information with
regard to the subject matter covered. It is sold with the understanding that the publisher is not engaged in rendering legal, accounting, or other professional advice. If
legal advice or other expert assistance is required, the services of a competent professional person should be sought.
—From a *Declaration of Principles* jointly adopted by a Committee of the
American Bar Association and a Committee of Publishers and Associations

Many of the designations used by manufacturers and sellers to distinguish their prod-
ucts are claimed as trademarks. Where those designations appear in this book and
Adams Media was aware of a trademark claim, the designations have been printed
with initial capital letters.

While all the stories in this book are true, some of the names, dates, and places have
been changed to protect anonymity.

This book is available at quantity discounts for bulk purchases.
For information, please call 1-800-872-5627.

My grandmother once said, "Find a man to take out the trash. Find a man to talk to. Find a man who's got a job. Find a man who's good in bed. Just make sure they never meet."

—DIANE SHADER SMITH

To *Mark,*
Micah,
Mallory,
Mel,
and *Flo*

Acknowledgments

MANY PEOPLE helped me in the process of researching, writing, and publishing this book. I would like to thank each of them for their contributions:

Mark, my husband, who encouraged me to tell the truth, however painful it might have been to him, for his support, his humor, his intellect, his writing, his editing, his handholding, but most of all, his unwavering love.

Micah and Mallory, my exceptional children, for tolerating my long hours.

Mel and Flo, my parents, for always supporting me.

Lori Conn, for suggesting I turn my interviews into a nonfiction book.

Harry Abrams and Maura Teitlebaum, my agents, who believed in my book even before *Desperate Housewives* made the subject of infidelity palatable to the American public. And to their associates, Beth Blickers, Mark Measures, and Alec Shankman, who worked with Harry and Maura to find the right home for this book.

Danielle Chiotti, my very talented editor, who shaped the book and made the journey an "E" ticket ride.

Katherine Hikel and Betsy Streisand, two extraordinary writers who helped me to the finish line with their words, their wit, and their wisdom.

Rabbi Karen Fox, the late Dr. Shirley Glass, Judge Lisa Hart, Dr. Ed Harris, Father Joseph Hernandez, Rabbi Steven Leder, Janet Lever, Brad Miller, Dr. Steven Reiter, and Dr. David Rimoin, for their professional expertise.

Lili Bosse, Ann Garber, Abigail Jones, Eric Lax, Julie Robinson, Deborah Sarokin, Amy Schiffman, and Ronit Stone, for taking the time to discuss this project with me and for sharing their opinions.

The team at Adams Media, my publisher, who supported Danielle and me at every turn: Scott Watrous, Gary M. Krebs, Beth Gissinger, Karen Cooper, Laura MacLaughlin, Paul Beatrice, and Daria Perreault.

Leigh Teresi and Audrey Spilker, for their speedy typing and editorial suggestions.

Cindy Cohen, my alibi, for getting me through the Nick phase and various other spots I have found myself in.

Nancy Sunkin, for taking my picture for the back cover.

And finally, to the wonderful women who entrusted me with their stories, for the privilege of retelling them.

Introduction

No one sat with me before my wedding and had "the talk." The talk where your mom, or your big sis, or your aunt says:

You're about to marry a man who is good looking, and tall, and kind, and smart, and he's going to be dedicated to the welfare of your children, and he's going to do everything he's supposed to do, and he's going to do it on time, and he's going to show up to your marriage every single day and every single night.

But you know what? One day you're going to be in the supermarket and you're going to accidentally bump into a can that's going to topple a whole stack of other cans and you're going to squat down and pick them up, and there's going to be a man helping you because it's such a mess. And he's going to smile at you, and you're going to smile back. And it's going to feel really good.

Or you'll be having some work done on your home and the contractor will be with you every day. One day he'll walk

through your kitchen and see that you're growing African vio-
lets on the windowsill and he'll bend over to look at the flowers
up close and he'll tell you they're really pretty. Those flowers
are important to you. You've put a lot of time and effort into
them. But nobody has ever noticed those flowers. Not your kids,
not your husband. But the contractor does.

You're going to start smelling cologne from outside your
marriage.

It might happen at a meeting. You make a comment and a
coworker says, "Wow, good idea! I never even thought of that."
You feel validated. Camaraderie at work is very seductive. You
might be lured by a scent, a glance, a smile, or a remark. You
don't dare acknowledge what's happening, or it will stir up
feelings—feelings you never expected to have after you walked
down the aisle.

I've been married for sixteen years to a man who is loving,
intelligent, kind, and handsome—a man who doesn't deserve
to be cheated on. But through a series of events, I found myself
dangerously attracted to another man.

Because of my own mixed feelings of attraction, guilt, and
longing, I became fascinated by the inner workings of extramarital affairs. I began asking questions: Are there any circumstances that would justify an affair? Are there men who deserve
to be cheated on? What if your husband cheats first? What if
your emotional needs aren't being met, or the passion is totally
gone? Is having an affair equivalent to marital suicide? I realized that to get the answers I wanted, I didn't need to talk to a
shrink or read a self-help book—I needed to talk to the women

who had done it. I wanted to know what these women gave up, what they'd gained, and if they would do it again.

So I started talking to women about their perception of the breakdown of fidelity in their marriages. I listened to them, and I recorded their stories on audiotape. The first thing I found out was that most women want more from their husbands than they're getting.

Angie wants her husband to turn off the TV and listen to her.

Meg loves to dance. It makes her feel young and special. She begs her husband to take her dancing, but he never does.

Lila has a husband who thinks he can control her. Not true.

Nancy's husband thinks she doesn't like sex. Also not true.

Susie is the butt of her husband's nasty remarks. In public. Every time they go out.

And so on, and so on. The complaints were endless. After a while, they started to blur.

Then I met Maria, and discovered a whole new side to the story. Maria was unique. She cheated because a handsome man had cast his eye upon her, leaving her heart aflutter and her panties moist. And then there was Talia, who was just bored. Nothing was particularly wrong at home—but the thought of kissing someone new was oh so exciting.

Is it wrong to yearn for that feeling?

Over the years, I've talked to women who have regrets, women who would give anything to go back, women who want to share their stories in hopes of preventing other women from feeling the devastating aftereffects of an extramarital affair.

I've also talked to women, such as Maria, whose affairs

didn't cause them any anguish, didn't lead to divorce, didn't end in doom and gloom; women whose affairs were fulfilling relationships that had nothing to do with their marriages; women who didn't want to leave their husbands because they enjoyed married life; women who wanted to stay because of their children; and women who were still enjoying their husbands *and* their lovers.

Their stories seduced me, leaving me envious of their ability to throw caution to the wind and curious as to how they did it—why they did it. A woman who engages in extramarital sex puts her own needs and desires before her husband's, a concept many women, myself included, find both baffling and compelling. When it comes to extramarital attraction, there's often an inner battle between the angel and the devil—between the "want to" and the "ought to."

Should we indulge our desire to spend time with a man who stokes the fire that had been banked, a man who simply looks good, smells great, and flatters our egos? Or should we focus our attention back on our marriages, those loving relationships so bogged down by the typical stresses of daily life that passion and sex take a back seat to mounting orthodontia bills, mortgage payments, and endless household chores?

Can a marriage that starts with love, sex, and passion endure the weathering of time? In talking to these women, I learned that every woman thinks about leaving her husband. Or cheating on him. At least once. A woman who says she's never thought about these things is either not married or in denial. Or she's too afraid to admit it. Married women of all ages have emotional and sexual needs, and if their needs aren't met at home they'll seek fulfillment elsewhere.

Why does a woman cheat? How does she keep her marriage intact? How does she face herself in the mirror each morning? Who is she thinking about when she makes love to her husband? What does she tell her children when she's not there for them? How does she endure the guilt of deception, and how does she cope with the fear of discovery?

There are no simple answers, but the women I spoke with did their best to address these questions. I learned that the reasons women cheat are as varied as the women themselves. Not only were their stories different, so were their accents, their styles of dress, and their socioeconomic status. I wanted you to meet these women and know them as I did. But to protect their identities, I have masked their names, hometowns, and family lives. In the editing of these stories, I have clarified areas that, in the telling, seemed vague or imprecise. I have generally kept the women's own language and vocabularies intact to retain the spirit and attitude of these amazing women.

We can learn from these women if we're willing to ask questions and listen to their answers. It's time to start a dialogue.

PART ONE

Dirty
Little
Secrets

1

1.

My Story

Part One

I AM A desperate housewife. Not like the ones on TV, but a real one, struggling to be a good wife, a good mother, a good daughter, a good friend, a good writer. I am also a short-order cook, on duty 24/7, serving various cuisines—Mediterranean for my husband Mark; red meat every two hours for our fourteen-year-old son, Micah; and four hot meals a day for our twelve-year-old daughter, Mallory. And then there are the kids' friends, who show up almost every day with their insatiable, and often picky, teenage appetites. Add a rambunctious white Lab, Dewey, and a demanding rescue kitty, Millie, and you'll understand why there's never a dull moment in my kitchen . . . nor a tidy one in the rest of my house. Sometimes I can handle all the balls I'm juggling; sometimes I just want to escape.

That's what I was hoping to do when I left for New York a few years back. Mark and I were happily married but had just received some crushing news: Our daughter, Mallory, who was three at the time, had been diagnosed with cystic fibrosis, a disease that would change all of our lives forever. After sobbing for three days, I boarded a plane to New York, hoping that throwing myself into work would provide a much-needed break from my distress and give me the perspective I needed to be strong for my family.

My excellent adventure with flirting began on that cross-country flight. Settling into my seat, I smiled to the good-looking man sitting next to me and he smiled back. Later, he made a quip about the news article I was reading, which led to some harmless banter. He introduced himself as Nick Livingston. Turned out he lived in LA, too. When he ordered a drink for himself and one for me, I felt a rush of excitement. We spent the next five hours sharing intimate details of our lives. He was the gorgeous stranger I would never see again. Or so I thought. It never occurred to me that I'd be bringing home more baggage than I left with.

When we landed, Nick invited me to dinner and pressed me for my phone number. I told him I already had plans, so he suggested we have a drink the next night. Because of my unwavering belief that you don't have sex with men other than your husband, I didn't see any harm in meeting him for an hour. One hour turned into four, and at the end of the evening he invited me back to his hotel room. I was shocked, wondering what signals I had given off that could have led him to think that sleeping together was even a possibility. I let him know I was flattered, but I declined.

Back in my hotel room, the thoughts whirling in my head kept me from falling asleep. Nick was so charming, so interesting, so utterly attractive. Being with him felt really great, but also unsettling. Why was I thinking about this man when I had a wonderful husband at home who was satisfying in so many ways? It was all so confusing. Mark and I never kept secrets from each other. . . . How would I respond when he asked about the trip? Should I mention meeting Nick? How could I, when just thinking about Nick sent my heart spinning? I tried to convince myself that this was an innocent flirtation—just something to help me forget the pervasive sadness that enveloped our lives—and finally drifted off.

*Why was I thinking about this man when I had
a wonderful husband at home who was satisfying in so many ways?*

After the trip, the reality of Mallory's diagnosis started to sink in. It was a terribly difficult time for all of us, and it sparked a pivotal change in my marriage. During the day, things were just as they'd always been—my responsibilities as wife, mother, and writer distracted me from my worries. But at night, things were different. Mark and I were so crazed by Mal's treatments—and our own fears—that we fell into bed each night, too exhausted for romance of any kind. Questions tortured us: What kind of childhood would Mallory have? Would she ever get married? Would she be able to have children? Or—the most horrifying thought of all—would she need to be buried by her parents?

About a week after I returned from New York, my pager went off. I didn't recognize the number. Returning the page, I was surprised to hear Nick say hello. He invited me to meet him for a midafternoon coffee. It was so easy to say yes. But after hanging up, I was saddled with guilt. I called Mark at work to fill him in on my day. "Just on my way out to run some errands and then I'm going to meet a friend for coffee," I said.

Nick *was* just a friend, I was sure of it. So why hadn't I told Mark who I was meeting? "Duh," I said aloud to no one. This was no accidental omission; I meant to keep the date a secret. It had to stay that way, at least for now.

Desperate times call for desperate measures, so I launched into full beauty mode. I called Daniel, my hairdresser, and begged him for a 9:30 appointment. He was way overscheduled, but hearing the urgency in my voice, he reluctantly squeezed me in. From there I went straight to Neiman Marcus for an 11:00 makeover at the Bobbie Brown counter. Forty-five minutes later, with eyes and lips lined and cheeks blushed, I was feeling like a whole new woman.

At noon, I sailed through the doors of a trendy boutique, looking for an outfit that matched my mood. The shopping gods were smiling on me that day; on display was the answer to my prayers—a pair of tight winter-white jeans and a slinky chiffon top. I charged the whole outfit, including a necklace the sales girl recommended.

By 1:30 I was standing in front of my mirror at home, surveying the results. I looked good. I felt good. I was ready.

At 2:30 sharp, I was seated at Starbucks, hoping that a half-hour reading magazine articles would calm me down. It didn't. I was a nervous wreck, vacillating between wanting to see Nick and wanting to get up and leave. With a husband at work and two kids at school, why did I feel like I was back in junior high?

Around ten of three, Nick walked in, clean-shaven and natty. When he leaned over to give me a quick kiss on the lips, he smelled delicious. He was wearing Tuscany, my favorite men's cologne. His relaxed manner stood in marked contrast to the way I felt. We sat for more than two hours, talking about our work, my children, and recent movies—everything but my husband. It all seemed harmless enough—until he invited me to dinner the following night.

I desperately wanted to accept. But dinner could be dangerous. Dinner definitely fell into the "date" category. I told him I'd try to free my schedule and call him in the morning. We walked together out to our cars. This time I leaned over and kissed him on the cheek.

Back in my car, I sprang into action and started making calls; I was a woman on a mission. I needed a convincing story to tell Mark. I needed someone to cover for me. And I needed a babysitter.

My first call was to Cindy, a lifelong friend, to see if she would be my alibi. "No problem," she said, "as long as Mark doesn't call me. I don't want to have to lie to him." I was pretty sure Mark wouldn't check up on me—I had never given him any reason to doubt me. Yet.

Returning home, it appeared that my family life was moving along as usual, completely unaffected by my inner turmoil. The kids were home; Micah was playing on the computer and Mallory was playing with her toys. Dinnertime was fast approaching, but I was too wound up to deal with my usual domestic duties. Since the kids were occupied, I went upstairs and jumped on the treadmill to burn off some energy before Mark got home.

Later that night, when Mark was reading in bed, I launched my plan: "I'd like to take Cindy to dinner tomorrow night. She's been going through a lot of stuff lately." Mark didn't mind at all, and even offered to come home a little earlier than usual to get dinner together. "You're such a good friend," he said. "Cindy is lucky to have you, and so am I." I waited until Mark was fast asleep, then I got out of bed quietly and tiptoed downstairs to call Nick to confirm our date. It could have waited until the next day, but I really wanted to hear his voice again before going to sleep. My dreams were oh so sweet.

I chose Chez Jay for our rendezvous because of its dark anonymity. As soon as we sat down, Nick ordered a bottle of Duckhorn Cabernet. Eating with Nick was safe, it seemed, because we weren't going to have a physical relationship. But when I opened the menu and saw the price of the wine—more than $100—it occurred to me that this might be the beginning of a well-planned seduction.

From across the table, Nick openly appraised my outfit—a sexy, sheer camisole under an uncharacteristically tight sweater with a plunging neckline—and reached for my hand. Then he rubbed his leg against mine.

Safe? Who was I kidding? Throughout dinner I felt an addicting combination of arousal and trepidation. We leaned in close, talking about everything. As he told me about all the traveling he did for work, and all the sleeping . . . alone . . . in hotels . . . it became clear he was a man with needs. I was in trouble. But as it turned out, the end of the evening was anticlimactic, at best. When Nick walked me to the car, he didn't even try to kiss me good night. I drove off, not knowing whether to feel relieved or disappointed.

When I got home, I checked on the kids. As I kissed each of them on their foreheads, I thought of Mark waiting upstairs. Would he know? Would he be able to see it on my face?

I found Mark in the bedroom watching *The Terminator.* Again. "Don't you ever get sick of that movie?" I asked, sounding shrewish. "Nope," Mark said. "I love the story. It's how I escape." I softened a bit. Who was I to be judgmental? Wasn't I using Nick in the same way?

As I settled into bed I babbled for a few minutes about Cindy's "problems," hoping I didn't sound as guilty as I felt. Fortunately, Mark, ever trusting, went right to sleep. I lay awake for hours, replaying the evening with Nick in my head again and again.

Over the next few weeks, Nick called me almost every day, and I lived for those stolen moments. He never said anything overtly sexual, but each time he called, I held the phone with sweaty palms, feeling giddy, anxious, aroused. One afternoon, Mark surprised me by coming home early while I was on the phone. "Say hi to Nick for me," he said, laying his briefcase casually on the kitchen table. My heart stopped. How the hell did Mark know about Nick?

Mark poured himself a Scotch and went upstairs to do some work. I wasn't ready for a confrontation, so I busied myself around the house, trying to organize my thoughts. Finally, when I couldn't stand it any longer, I dragged myself upstairs. "Who do you think Nick is, anyway?" I asked, trying to sound relaxed. Mark gave me a quick glance, then turned back to his work.

"Some guy you met on your trip to New York." His voice was calm and even. I stood there, speechless and panicked, while several beats of heavy silence passed between us.

I was an idiot—I had fooled myself into thinking that because I wasn't paying my usual attention to Mark—asking about his day, demanding we talk in bed at night—he wasn't paying attention to me. Big mistake. My husband had radar ears. He didn't miss a thing.

Mark told me he'd seen Nick's card on my desk when he was looking for my address book. His voice was neutral, and his shoulders didn't display any anger or tension.

"Do you want me to tell you about him?" I asked.

"I already know enough," Mark said, finally turning to face me.

"He's just a friend," I said. I sounded unconvincing, even to myself.

Mark held two thumbs and two index fingers up in the sign of the "W" (our family code for "whatever") and turned back to his work. "Want to meet him?" I asked.

"What for?" he responded.

"So you can see that there's nothing to worry about." Even as the words came out, I knew that arranging for Mark to meet Nick would be a terrible mistake. But as it often happens, my emotions had clouded my judgment; I decided to forge ahead.

Cindy and her husband, Pat, and two other couples were coming to dinner the following Friday. Even though I knew I was playing with fire, I called Nick to invite him, under the guise that I wanted to introduce him to Rhonda, a recently divorced, flirtatious mother of two. Nick said that he wasn't up for a blind date but would love to meet my husband and children. I asked Nick to at least feign interest in Rhonda, for the sake of my marriage; he was happy to play the part of a potential suitor.

In the days leading up to the party, I ran around like a madwoman, buying flowers and wine, removing clutter from the corners, picking out a new outfit. Anxiety set in—would Nick like my home? Would my cooking impress him? Would our friends recognize my feelings for Nick? Would Mark? I convinced myself that Nick's cameo was a good thing. It would prove to Mark that Nick was just a friend, especially since I was setting him up with Rhonda.

Finally, Friday arrived.

Rhonda came early, and we opened a bottle of wine and sat at the kitchen table, sipping and chatting about Nick. It wasn't hard for me to talk him up. I was so animated that Rhonda said, "If I didn't know better, I'd think you had the hots for him."

"I'm married," I insisted, "happily married." *Are my feelings that obvious?* I made a mental note to tone it down.

The doorbell rang and my heart stopped. What if it was Nick? But it wasn't. As our friends arrived, I ushered them inside, attempting to make small talk, all the while waiting eagerly for Nick. He was the last to show up. When he finally did, I let Mark answer. Nick greeted Mark with a warm handshake and a bottle of Glenlivet.

Then Nick walked over to me and handed me a gorgeous bouquet of red roses, which were completely over the top, considering the circumstances. "Beautiful flowers for a beautiful hostess," he said. Mark caught the remark and rolled his eyes. Nick's comment hung in the air like a scarlet letter.

To divert everyone's attention, I steered Nick over to Rhonda.

During cocktails, Nick worked the room with amazing poise. Though he was among strangers, he had them all in the palm of his hand within minutes. I bustled about, playing the gracious hostess but all the while I was watching him. He winked at me a few times when our eyes met from across the room. The thrill of danger was intoxicating.

At dinner, Mark made a point of sitting next to Nick and chatting him up about his work and his travel, which wasn't part of my plan. Cindy grabbed the seat on Nick's other side, shutting out a visibly disappointed Rhonda. I threw Cindy a dirty look. Throughout dinner, I felt like I was sitting on a powder keg. Every time anyone asked Nick a question, I took another large sip of my wine. It was looking like a four-Advil night.

After dinner, Rhonda made a beeline for the couch and beckoned Nick over. She'd been to the powder room and freshened her face. Once Nick was beside her, she asked him to help her remove her jacket, revealing a black bra top. The two of them were doing the giggly flirting routine. I busied myself with hostessing, but it bothered me that she was making such an obvious play for him. It also bothered me that Nick walked Rhonda to her car at the end of the night. That was the moment I realized how deep in I was.

In bed that night, Mark and I played my favorite post-party game: reviewing the evening scene by scene. Of course, the only thing I really cared about was his reaction to Nick and me. Luckily, Mark didn't suspect a thing. From his vantage point, the dinner party had been a huge success. He praised me for a great job, gave me a kiss, rolled over, and went to sleep.

I should have been relieved that my attraction to Nick had gone unnoticed, but instead I tossed and turned, trying to get the picture of Nick flirting with Rhonda out of my head. Had he kissed her good night when he walked her to her car? Would he call her to ask her out? I knew I had no right to be possessive—Nick wasn't my husband! Still, it left me feeling disturbed.

The next morning, after dropping the kids at school, I headed straight for Cindy's house to do some recon. She'd hardly opened her front door before I started interrogating her. "And good morning to you, too," she said. I asked her why she'd sat next to Nick at dinner.

"I figured it was my last chance to get to know him before you slept with him," she said.

"Is it that obvious?"

Cindy just smiled.

"I'm in over my head," I admitted.

Cindy didn't see it that way. "Nah, you'll get over it," she said as she ushered me into the living room.

"So, what do you think of him?" I asked as we sat down.

"He's fabulous. I totally get it," she said. We were silent for a minute.

"Shit!" I said.

Nick didn't ask Rhonda out. Instead, he called me that afternoon to thank me for dinner and to invite me for cocktails after work. This time I came up with a lame PTA-related excuse for Mark, and met Nick at 6:30. I was getting careless, but it didn't matter. I needed to see him. We shared a pitcher of margaritas and when we were completely looped, he invited me on a road trip. Nick wanted to visit a girlfriend who lived near my sister, Meryl—the perfect excuse. As soon as he mentioned it, I knew I was in. But how to explain it to Mark?

In bed that night, with the lights off, I broached the subject.

"Nick had an interesting idea. He wants to visit a girlfriend up north and I've wanted to give Meryl Micah's old dresser. He suggested we drive up together."

Even though we weren't touching, I felt Mark's body tense. "You gotta be kidding. You hate road trips."

"But this is important. I'd be doing my sister a huge favor."

He sighed. "What about the kids?" I knew from his tone that he was upset, but I pushed it a bit further.

"I thought we could do it the weekend you and Micah have the Cub Scout overnight. I'll take Mallory with me."

Mark seemed resigned. "I'm not going to tell you no, but I'm not happy about this."

"Thank you, Mark. This means a lot to me—and it will to Meryl, too."

What the hell was I thinking? How could I possibly do this to Mark? Then again, what was it that I was supposedly doing? Nick and I weren't sleeping together. Was it a crime to have a male friend?

I had this conversation with myself over and over, as if by thinking about it enough I would come up with the desired answer: that I wasn't doing anything wrong.

But I was. Nick wasn't my lover but he might as well have been. He was so much more than a friend, and what I gave him was so much more intimate than sex. He was the perfect escape from the drudgery of my daily life. It was Nick I thought about as I walked on the treadmill, Nick I wanted to call after I'd heard a great joke, Nick with whom I wanted to share my random victories.

Physically, I was home every night with my husband and children. But emotionally, I was absent. Any shrink would have told me I was absolutely cheating on Mark, even if I didn't want to believe it, or deal with the reason why.

And there was a reason—Mallory's diagnosis. Until then, I had been the happily married mother and wife. Mark and I had a model marriage. Our first date was on a Sunday evening and a month later we were engaged. When we announced our engagement, friends would tease, "I didn't even know you had a boyfriend."

Mark was always there for me, never more so than the day the doctor told us that the six-month-old fetus I was carrying—our third child—had cystic fibrosis. Several doctors told me to terminate, that CF was a deadly disease that no child should have to endure. I took their advice and then cried myself to sleep for a week, mourning the loss of a baby girl I had desperately wanted.

A week later, we found out that Mallory also had CF. This time, everyone said, "Don't worry, they're close to finding a cure. Babies with CF used to die before their fifth birthday, but now they live into their early thirties." My heartache was indescribable.

The following year, at the age of thirty-eight, I found blood in my bra. A biopsy showed breast cancer—ductal carcinoma in situ. The bad cells were so widespread that the only option was mastectomy. I was horrified. What would happen to me once I no longer had breasts? Would my husband still find me attractive? Would I still feel sexual? Mark promised me that I would be just as beautiful to him after mastectomy as before, so I opted for a double with immediate reconstruction.

Once again, Mark stood by my side every step of the way. More important, he loved me just as much when it was all over as he had before the nightmare started. And the following year, when Micah was diagnosed with Tourette Syndrome, Mark put on a happy face and became Micah's constant companion, taking him and friends on snowboarding trips and train adventures. He was the perfect Disneyland Dad.

But it was hard for *me* to have fun with Mark because looking at him was like looking in the mirror—he couldn't save me since we were both drowning in the same ocean of grief.

Nick, on the other hand, helped me forget my problems. He seduced me with his *joie de vivre* and his carefree smile. I liked how I felt when I was with him, but even more, I liked how I didn't feel—which was scared. Nick caught my eye, he took my breath away, and then he held my attention. I connected with him in a way that was deep, irresistible, and profoundly confusing.

That confusion was the impetus for this book. I was conflicted about deriving pleasure from spending time with a man other than my husband. This wasn't supposed to happen. It wasn't anything I saw growing up. My mother and father are still in love after fifty years of marriage.

As my story with Nick played itself out, I began to wonder if there were other women grappling with this issue. I did some research and found that although millions of women are happily married, millions of others are betraying their husbands. I wanted to talk to some of these women.

I wasn't sure if any of them would want to talk to me.

Turns out they did.

Women in the market, at the gym, at baby showers, in coffee shops, at the hair salon—in all pockets of America—had a story to tell, or knew someone else who did. I got so many referrals that before I knew it, I had stacks of notebooks and taped interviews—more than enough material to fill a book. The interviewing process became a personal quest to find the resolution to my own predicament, which you'll read about at the end of this book.

These women, who were so generous with their time and with their truth, helped me find my way. I offer their stories so that other women can learn from their wisdom just as I have.

2.

The Secret Life of a Soccer Mom

The Story of Jennifer Faust

*J*ennifer Faust was one of the first women I spoke to on my journey of sex, lies, and audiotapes. A colleague at work introduced us. He said we had a lot in common—the soccer mom thing, a happy marriage, part-time work. I was hopeful she could supply me with some insights into taking the plunge.

Jennifer said the easiest place for us to talk would be in her car—a Range Rover—in which she looped the perimeter of her town several times each day between 3:30 and 6:30 P.M., ferrying her children to activities and running her errands. She was the model wife and mom: She was president of her PTA, she served hot lunch at school every day, and she kept the books for her husband's business.

A tall, poised blond in her mid-forties, Jennifer's turquoise eyes twinkled with empathy and good humor. She had bronzed *skin and an athletic figure. As she spoke, she gestured with her hands. Her wedding ring—the symbol of her commitment—glittered in the afternoon sunlight.*

Between drop-off and pickup for soccer practice, religious school, and Boy Scouts, Jennifer and I talked about life and love, and how her affair had restored her sense of beauty and self-esteem, which had been eroded through the years by her husband, Frank. Frank always told her she was attractive, but his lack of interest in the bedroom caused her to doubt it. Regardless, Frank had been a good husband in many other ways. Jennifer had been happily married for eighteen years, and hoped to live with her husband for at least as many more.

MAE WEST said, "I was Snow White, but I drifted." That's me. I can't blame it on my husband—he came home every single night, he was good to me, good to our children, and was a good companion. But still, I had an affair. If I had to give a reason why I cheated, I would say it's because our sex life was virtually nonexistent.

I've now been married longer than I was single. I met Frank in college. He was four years older, the brother of one of the girls in my dorm, and he used to come around in his VW bus and take a bunch of us out to the beach, or to a movie, and treat us to ice cream afterward. We'd all ride around in his bus, listening to music, talking, giggling, and getting to know the area—a great thing for those of us who were from out of town.

But Frank was no wild and crazy hippie. He was a clean-cut, straight-looking guy, enrolled in the engineering program. He worked for his dad, who was a structural engineer with his own firm. Engineers are wacky! They can, and will, tell you if your skirt is an eighth of an inch shorter in the back than in the front. Frank fit the mold—he was organized, regular, and precise.

I liked his sense of humor and the structure and safety he represented, especially since I'd grown up in a family that was a little looser around the edges. My father was a salesman, lively and loving, but he changed jobs often and we had some financial ups and downs while I was growing up; it seemed as if he was always trying to get ahead, but never did. My mother taught piano and acted in local theater, so she was always in and out of the house. I was the typical middle child, and that stayed with me into adulthood. As a result, I was looking for structure, and Frank—also a middle child—shared my view of the way we should live.

We both wanted to wait a while to have sex—I needed some time, to be sure about myself and my partner. A lot of the girls around me complained that the guys they dated just wanted to do it all the time, and didn't care about anything else. Frank wasn't pushy about sex; he respected me, and I thought I was lucky. He's a pretty private guy as well, and I respected that about him.

Frank and I got married the summer after I graduated, and that's when we lost our virginity together. It wasn't as bad as it sounds; we had both read books on sex. I'd gotten a lot of those as shower gifts—*The Joy of Sex* and whatnot—I looked at them, often, by myself. Once or twice we read them together. That was okay—Frank was a guy who went by the book. But he was sensitive, and the least little thing could make him lose his erection. It embarrassed me, too, as I thought this happened because I was doing something wrong or wasn't enough of a turn-on to keep him interested. It got a little better with time, as we got more familiar with each other, but sex was never a focal point of our marriage.

Two years after we married, I wanted to have a baby. We were away for the weekend and I was ovulating. I said, "It's time to make love. This is it!" Frank dutifully got himself into me and came very quickly; then he used a vibrator to get me off. This wasn't unusual for us. As soon as I came, he bounded out of bed, saying, "Come on, I'm famished. Let's go get some breakfast." It's been that way ever since; he jumps out of bed each morning, raring to start his day. I've always been glad that he liked his job but I wished he liked to linger more. I stay fit, I play tennis, and I take care of my appearance, but I spent many years doubting my sex appeal. It didn't seem natural that I had a stronger sex drive than my husband. Sex wasn't as important, I told myself, as being with a loving, kind, devoted husband.

It didn't seem natural that I had a stronger
sex drive than my husband.

We lived a picture-perfect life. We had a house on a quiet street with probably fifteen kids under the age of twelve. For years, there was a monthly block party on Sunday night. We'd all congregate on one of our front lawns, sitting around on beach chairs, drinking wine, sharing potluck, and telling funny stories about the kids.

It was at one of these gatherings that I heard about my son's first kiss. He would never have told me, but my neighbor did. Her daughter, Ashley, had been at a party with my son, Charlie, where they were playing spin the bottle. Ashley had seen Charlie lock lips with one of the other girls. The very night I heard about this kiss I tucked Charlie into bed and asked him if he'd liked it. "Yeah," he grinned. "I didn't think I'd like it, but I did." I was happy for him but wistful that Frank and I didn't really kiss anymore. Life went on, and in many ways, it wasn't so bad.

After ten years of marriage, and three children, I met the doctor.

It was a Sunday morning, and I was cutting up watermelon for a party later that day. The knife slipped and I cut my palm. I couldn't get it to stop bleeding, so I called my doctor, but he was out of town. I got the young physician on call. Right away I liked the tone of reassurance and good humor in his voice. He told me over the phone that I should wrap my hand in a towel and then meet him in his office. Frank had taken the kids out, so I drove myself, with my hand all wrapped up.

There was no receptionist at his office when I got there, so I took a seat against the wall to wait. It was hot—the building's air conditioning must have been off—and I was starting to sweat. I unbuttoned a couple of buttons on my blouse, and I was dabbing at my cleavage with a hankie when the doctor arrived, walking briskly toward me with a boyish grin on his face. He was wearing a Yankees baseball cap, blue jeans, and a T-shirt. He introduced himself as Jeff, and apologized for his clothes, saying he'd been at the hardware store when he got the page. As I started to button up my blouse, he smiled and said, "Oh, don't worry about that—we're casual around here, as you can see."

He led me down the corridor into an exam room, where he gently unwrapped the towel and looked at my wound. I saw that he had a gold band on his left ring finger, and that there was dirt under his nails. He said that he was going to have to put in some sutures. I asked, "How much is this gonna hurt?" He grinned and said, "One man's pain is another man's pleasure."

As he prepared to sew me up, I looked around the exam room and was surprised to see from his diploma that we'd gone to the same college and were about the same age. He cleaned and anesthetized the wound, then stitched it, carefully, with finesse. His hands were handsome and shapely; I felt assurance and gentleness in their touch. You can tell a lot about how a man will be in bed by the way he uses his hands; I was surprised to catch myself thinking that way. I watched his face, youngish, well sunned, confident, as he concentrated on his work. I wanted to say something that would establish a connection of some sort, but I just sat there silent, hoping he wouldn't notice the beads of sweat that had formed on my forehead. I was on edge, unnerved, a little jumpy; maybe it was the adrenaline from the injury, or maybe it was being near a very attractive man. He seemed amused by the whole thing. Then he walked me over to the front desk, shook my hand, and said goodbye.

Two weeks later, he called to ask how my stitches were. It seemed unusual for a doctor to check back in this way, especially since I had the kind of stitches that were going to fall out on their own, but I figured he was new in practice and was probably hustling to get patients. There was an awkward moment when neither of us said anything, so finally I said I had to go pick up my son. I didn't see the doctor for six months, until I injured a finger during a tennis game. Instead of calling my regular doctor, I made an appointment to see him.

While he was examining my hand, he told me he liked the color polish I was wearing. I mentioned that we had gone to the same school, nodding in the direction of his diploma.

We talked about our impressions of university life and what we had done after college. Somehow we segued into our marriages. He had been with his wife for six years but didn't have any children because she wasn't ready to take that step.

At some point the nurse popped her head in and said the patients were getting backed up. I stood up. He leaned in to give me a hug and say goodbye. We stood pressed full-length against each other. I could feel him hardening against me through our clothes. He didn't move, and I didn't move, and I stood there holding him, completely aroused. It was incredible. Something in my female spirit responded to this man in a way that was totally new to me. Gradually he loosened his hold; he smiled into my eyes, and without saying a word, left the room. I gathered up my purse and my coat, and went to the office to pay my bill. The nurse had my chart in front and pulled from it a prescription that she handed to me, saying it was to reduce the swelling. At the top of the slip of paper was Jeff's beeper number with a note saying I should call him anytime.

I felt the heat rising to my face, but the nurse didn't seem to notice. I jammed the paper into my pocket and ran out to my car. On the way home, I stopped at the mall to walk around and compose myself in the air-conditioned serenity of the shops. A display in the window of a lingerie boutique caught my eye. The store was a sensual maze, drawing me in with lush offerings of satin and frothy lace, impossible not to touch and desire. I tried on a bra-and-thong set, in black lace; it felt like a caress. I looked at myself in the mirror of the soft-lit dressing room, imagining Jeff's hands exploring the nuances of fabric, and felt flushed and aroused. I pushed thoughts of Jeff out of my head with a reminder: "You are a married woman!"

I quickly got dressed and paid for my purchases—they were more expensive than my usual underwear. I mumbled something about "my husband . . ." at the clerk, who eyed me with a "yeah, right" kind of look. All the while, the paper with Jeff's number was burning a hole in my pocket. Outside the store, I pulled it out, looked at it, and walked toward a trash can to get rid of it. Of course, I didn't.

That night, I soaked in a warm bath, powdered and perfumed myself, and put on my new black lace seduction garb under a white silk robe. I got into bed with a magazine. Frank came in, sniffed—he notices everything about me—and said, "You smell terrific, Jen!" To my surprise, he stripped to his shorts and slid in beside me, kissing and nibbling me on my neck and ears. It was so unlike him to be the initiator.

I slipped out of my robe, revealing the new black lace undies. His response was all I could have hoped for—we rolled around and laughed and panted and giggled, and had an unusually long and satisfying session, but the entire time we were making love I was fantasizing about Jeff. I remembered the crumpled-up prescription with his phone number on it, still in my pocket.

I held out for a couple of long, virtuous days, then I dialed his number.

The handsome young doctor started coming to my house on Mondays, the day my housekeeper had off, when my husband was at work. It was great because we'd both been tested, so no condoms were required. When we got upstairs, he would see how many different ways he could make me come before entering me. We found plenty, all new to me, and things my husband would never have thought of. Despite the comment he'd made about pain the first time we met, this man was totally into pleasure. He would bring lovely scented oil that he would massage into my thighs, taking his time and making me wait before unleashing the pleasure of full intercourse. I had multiple orgasms this way. We spent hours experimenting in the guest room. He would even help me change the sheets before he left. "Until next time," he'd say with a foxy grin.

The doctor had a very busy practice, but I wanted sex with him as often as we could squeeze it in. Sometimes I would drop off the kids, get my nails done, go out and buy a sexy thong, and wriggle into it before meeting him in his parking lot during lunch, for a hot make-out session in my car, where we'd tease each other with our fingers like a couple of teenagers.

I don't think my husband had any inkling of what was going

on. Sometimes I'd swing by Frank's office before meeting Jeff, just to check on Frank and tell him—more or less—where I was going. Even though it was always a lie, he never caught on. All he said was, "Go on, have fun. I'll see you at home." Sometimes I think he seemed a little relieved, as my secret life with Jeff took the pressure off him to perform. He seemed happy just to get into bed at night, watch TV, and fall asleep snoring in my ear. For me, it was sweetness all around, a near-perfect arrangement.

One afternoon, I was unexpectedly free, as my kids had play dates, so I stopped by the doctor's office. I had come from a board meeting at the school, and was dressed in a trim pink suit and matching high heels. He had just finished with a patient. He swept me into his private office and opened the door to a little storage room, filled with old files and boxes and equipment. In that dark room he pinned me against the wall for a quickie.

How we had sex never really mattered—I loved it every which way.

One day, after I'd been away with my family for a week, Jeff didn't answer my page. Several days passed and I tried again. He called me back this time, but said he wouldn't be free for another week. This surprised me, so I asked him why. He gave me some lame excuse, but when I pressed him about it, he admitted he'd been seeing someone else. I was sad because the relationship had been so pleasurable. And it was difficult to taper off my sexual desire after it was over. I craved his body, I longed for his touch, but most of all I missed his smell. In my tote bag I kept a T-shirt he'd worn. I couldn't help pulling it out, in secret, and inhaling the scent that had aroused me so.

Sometimes I buried my face in that shirt, and wept for what I knew was irretrievably gone.

But my other life beckoned me back, so I tended my gardens, participated in school events, and played a lot of tennis. The only clue I had that my husband noticed anything different was that after I stopped seeing Jeff, Frank said, mildly, "Aren't you becoming a bit of a homebody these days?" I hadn't realized how much time the affair with Jeff had taken up. Our family life continued, apparently unaffected by my little bout of self-indulgence. The only person who knew about my adventures was a woman from my book club, to whom I confessed after we read *The Bridges of Madison County*. She laughed and said she'd had a lover, too.

I read a lot back then. Romance novels, self-help books . . . anything that would take my mind off the doctor. I didn't miss him, but I did miss the excitement of our trysts. My sex life with Frank was humdrum and routine. I'd try little things to jazz it up—racy underwear, sexy magazines, X-rated videos. Frank would go along, as if to humor me, but I could tell that he hated most if it. "It seems so fake, Jen," he said.

One night I even made Frank take a love-and-sex quiz in *Cosmo*, which got him laughing but didn't do anything to improve our communication, or his desire. Frank and I had different levels of need. Being with the doctor, with his matter-of-fact enjoyment of the physical side of life, had given me the confidence to approach Frank about doing something to improve our sex life. To my surprise, he agreed. We found an amazing "sex therapist"; she made talking about everything really fun and easy. She opened up the discussion without intruding upon our sense of privacy. I see now that the program was "engineered" with a series of logical steps, and both Frank and I felt right at home within that structure.

Our "homework" was always very sexy. She would give us assignments—role-playing, sex toys, clothing—things that I would have been up for but that Frank would have thought way too kinky, and that would have made him nervous or embarrassed. But since the therapist required follow-through and follow-up, he'd do it.

Frank's natural inhibitions slowly melted away under the therapist's permissive guidance, and the fact that Frank was attracted to her added spice and intrigue to our sessions. As in all good therapy, the really good stuff happened after we left the office, giving us something to look forward to after each appointment. I can only imagine what went on in Frank's private sessions with the therapist. (She also met with each of us separately.)

All I know is that things started improving between us. Frank's shyness was disappearing, and he was into pleasures that I'd only hoped for in our earlier days. He was taking his time, he was more interested and less inhibited, and rarely leaped out of bed to go to work after we made love. Frank was now the one booking weekend getaways for the two of us. Finally, things were going the way I'd always longed for.

I assumed that I was done sleeping with other men.

But just last week a man named Cliff walked into my Pilates class. He's way too young for me, but there's something about him. The big surprise is he asked me to have a drink with him next week after class. I said yes, and haven't slept since.

3.

The Laws of Attraction

The Story of Dina Jackson

*M*y curiosity led me to a seminar called "Cheating Spouses: Do You Have One?" It was led by a Dick Tracy–type who specialized in surveillance. Three hours into the all-day event, I approached the lectern to ask the speaker for a referral to a cheating spouse. He wasn't willing to introduce me to any of his clients, saying they wouldn't appreciate a call from me. I pressed harder, telling him that there's a lot of this going around and that I didn't need to know them, just their stories. I promised that none of their identities would be compromised. The guy thought about it for a minute and then said he knew a woman—not a client, but a friend—who might want to talk. I knew by his description that Dina Jackson was going to be my kind of gal—lively, confident, powerful.*

Dina was a partner in one of Chicago's most prestigious law firms. When I arrived at her office, an old stone building with a view of the lake, the receptionist greeted me, and then buzzed for Dina's assistant to take me to her. Dina was on the phone, and motioned for me to sit on the sofa. She was a buff, elegant woman in a persimmon suit that complemented her warm brown skin, and black heels that accentuated her regal posture. Her dark hair was woven into a cascade of tiny braids.

Behind her desk was a credenza, which had on it an old black-and-white photo of a diner with a sign hanging outside that said "Whites Only." There were also some framed family photos on her desk and a picture of Dina and several other women seated in a river raft. I smelled an interesting fragrance, which turned out to be incense burning in a brass holder.

On the phone, Dina was smooth and personable, clearly having fun, alternately asserting herself and playfully foxing the person on the other end into giving her what she wanted. Dina's assistant brought in a pot of coffee, which she placed on the table next to the sofa, and then walked out, closing the door behind her. Dina, still talking, motioned for me to help myself. I reached for the pot and poured out two cups, just as she was hanging up the phone. Lifting the creamer, I asked, "How do you take yours?" "Black, like me," Dina said with a wink. Then she rose from her chair and came over to sit next to me. She sized me up and then spontaneously gave me a hug. "This is going to be great fun," she said. I turned on the tape recorder and settled back into the plush leather couch to hear her story.

∞

∞

I GOT MARRIED at twenty-seven, and what the hell did I know? The church required us to see Father Reilly for premarital counseling sessions. Malcolm thought the sessions were a waste of time and gave Father Reilly the business about everything. Every time the priest asked Malcolm a question, Malcolm would question him right back—not in a negative way, but pointed and skeptical.

One of the questions Father Reilly asked Malcolm was how he would feel if his wife earned more money than he did.

"A black man's sense of masculinity don't come from his paycheck, if you know what I mean," Malcolm said, clearly secure in his sexuality. I blushed. So did Father Reilly. But he never brought it up again. I was proud of my man.

Malcolm and I met at a huge ritzy wedding—I knew the bride, and he knew the groom. There was a band and dancing, and Malcolm could shake his booty. I'd had a lot of champagne and was feeling frisky, and—even though I knew it was risky behavior—we ended up back at my place. He stayed for a week.

I was starved for affection. I hadn't been touched, really touched, in what seemed like forever. I was so busy with law school that my love life and my sex life were nonexistent. Love could wait; it was a demand I couldn't handle. There were other priorities—finishing law school, where I had worked really hard, and keeping myself to a demanding schedule of study so that

I'd do well. I was at the top of my class, on *Law Review*, on the student advisory committee, active in the Women in Law Society—all of it.

So Malcolm was a very welcome distraction from my academic life. The first morning he was there, he slipped out of bed, went to the kitchen, whipped up breakfast—and served it to me in bed on a tray. I was still a little hung-over, but flabbergasted. No man had ever cooked this way for me—waffles, fruit, tea, a flower across the plate—the whole bit. And the fruit, it wasn't just cut up, it was shaped, arranged. He'd folded the napkin into a flower as well. I asked him where he learned to do all that, and he laughed. He was a cook, he said, at one of the upscale restaurants in the city, enrolled part-time in a culinary arts program. He was working his way up to executive chef, hoping to have a restaurant of his own—or a bunch of 'em—someday.

I was nuts about Malcolm's look. He was muscular and athletic, medium height, with his hair in little dreads, gold hoops in his ears, and a big infectious grin—kind of a Rasta pirate. He came from a distressed background, quite different from my family and their middle-class, professional roots. Breaking away from his beginnings, he had made his way on his own, finishing high school—barely—and talking a lot of street slang. But he was very bright, and eager to get ahead. He said his grandmother had taught him the love of food and the art of cooking when he was very young. He left home when she died; he was seventeen. "If I hadn't gotten a job in a restaurant right then, I'd be dealing drugs right now," he used to say to me.

Malcolm was totally supportive of my heavy study schedule. He paid attention to me so completely—to my likes and dislikes, my moods, my needs. How could I not fall for him? Sex was always incredible with him. He was never in a rush, and pleasing me was his mission every time we made love.

Malcolm's own schedule was as demanding as mine—early mornings, late nights, weekends, and always the pressure to perform, impress your superiors, curry favor, work to get ahead. And, unlike a lot of chefs who eat, drink, and smoke to excess—an occupational hazard—he took care of himself and worked out.

Malcolm was talented and ambitious. Watching people's reactions to food was his great pleasure. When my friends or associates would come by to drop off a brief or whatever, Malcolm would sit them down and say, "Just try a little bite of this before you go," and people would go, *Oh, mmmm!* Whatever it happened to be—soup, roast pork, a sliver of pâté—he'd make a presentation of it. People adored having his little treats, and he loved giving pleasure—he was the same way in bed.

We always stayed at my place, and Malcolm did so much for me that I was happy to have him around. It turned out the reason we never went to his place was that he didn't really have a place; he'd been staying with a friend, another chef, who also had a busy schedule. Malcolm had his stuff stashed there, but had never really unpacked. He'd landed there after a breakup with another woman he'd been living with; she couldn't take his schedule, so she found another lover and kicked him out.

Taking Malcolm in seemed like one thing I could do for him. I was already lined up for a job where I'd be making about twice as much as he was. When he moved his belongings to my place, I was surprised at how little he had—a couple of duffel bags, a box of cookbooks, a set of knives. That was it. When

I suggested looking for another place together, he said, "Baby, what's wrong with this? Save your good money for a while. Then we'll see what happens." I thought that was logical. We could always do the household thing together later—you know, pick out curtains, china, that kind of stuff. Create a home together. I didn't realize that I had a roving gypsy on my hands.

I was very happy when Malcolm asked me to marry him. We had our wedding two weeks after graduation. It was a simple affair, our families and a few friends, at Our Lady of Perpetual Help. Father Reilly celebrated the wedding and said Mass. We had a small afternoon reception in my aunt's back-yard. A bunch of Malcolm's chef pals got together and made a wonderful barbecue. We were so happy, and everyone seemed happy for us.

We spent our wedding night at a five-star hotel. It was a soft, rainy night, with a certain melancholy that made you want to linger in bed. I'd always fantasized about what my wedding night would be like—but reality was way better. We didn't get out of bed for two days.

I spent the summer studying for the bar while Malcolm worked in the restaurant at night and took classes during the days. After I took the exam, we spent a few weeks in Puerto Vallarta, finally getting the honeymoon we had wanted. The hotel screwed up our reservation, so I started joking around with the clerk about messing things up, saying I didn't want this to jinx our marriage. They felt bad, so they upgraded us to this fantastic two-story suite. We had a bathtub big enough for us to lie down in together—side by side! At night, I would light candles in the bathroom and fill the tub with steaming bubbles, and we would lie in there, touching each other gently, until we couldn't stand it any longer. It was all so beautiful with the moonlight and warm breeze on the balcony overlooking the ocean. The bar exam results were hanging over my head, but most of the time I was distracted by all that great sex!

Malcolm got to know the chefs at the resort, and, of course, they invited him into the kitchen. Before I knew it, he had the kitchen crew whipping up special dishes for us and bringing them to our table. One of them invited us to visit his home, in a village an hour or so away. I knew it was going to be a food-chef-cooking expedition, so I told Malcolm to go ahead without me. I was exhausted, and just wanted to lie in the sun and relax. Little did I know he wouldn't be back till late the next day. Of course, I believed him when he said they'd just visited the guy's hometown, eaten a bunch of meals at all the relatives' houses, and slept at his mother's place—a matter of etiquette, he said. I should have known right then that there'd be trouble down the road. I mean, what kind of guy goes away by himself overnight on his honeymoon? That was Malcolm; cooking came first. It worked for me—something about those flavors got his juices flowing, and he came back horny as hell. Our honeymoon was really great—definitely worth the wait!

When we got back home, I still had the bar results hanging over my head. If I brought up my anxiety, Malcolm would express absolute confidence in me. "You the smartest woman I ever met," he said. "No way you didn't pass! You're gonna make one hell of a lawyer."

I did pass, and then my first year at the firm was over in a flash. I got a great annual review and a big pay raise. I was making more than twice as much as Malcolm, but he didn't seem to care; he was glad not to have to worry about money and he had confidence in his own prospects.

My firm invited me to sit on the recruiting committee. Most people considered that to be a plum job. You got to travel—visiting law schools to interview promising students—and during July and August you had an unlimited expense account to wine and dine the summer associates. I was very proud of myself.

Naturally, the restaurant where Malcolm worked got a lot of our trade. I never told the lawyers I took there that the handsome chef with the big smile who came out to check on our table was my husband. By that point, Malcolm had been promoted to head line cook, and he was very busy, taking on more and more duties and staying out late—sometimes all night. Often the only time I would see him was at the restaurant.

The first thing the committee did after I joined it was to assign me to mentor a new black associate named Brian. I knew Brian by sight from law school—he had graduated a year ahead of me. He had applied to the firm and was accepted, but he had deferred his start date for two years to do pro bono voter registration in the Deep South. He was starting his law career one year after me, and it was my job to introduce him around and show him the ropes. During Brian's first few days at the firm, I explained billable hours, partnership politics, and other inner workings of the firm. As I sat across from him at lunch one day, I thought, "He's smart and personable . . . and sure not bad to look at." He was polished and groomed, quite tall, with a thoughtful, serious manner. I knew his family background was a lot like mine. But Brian was married, and so was I, so I didn't give it too much thought. He was just a familiar black face in an overwhelmingly white firm.

Over the next few months, Brian and I developed a very comfortable rapport. We conferred often during the day, helping each other with our cases when we could, or trading tales of comic woe about the life of a lowly law firm associate. We had lunch together. We spent a lot of evenings in the office—everyone did. I still liked having sex with Malcolm, but our nights together were increasingly infrequent. During the days, I was working hard but enjoying it more thanks to having Brian around.

Eventually, Malcolm and I started doing occasional evening and weekend activities as a foursome with Brian and his wife, Janelle—a dinner here, a movie there. Janelle and Malcolm had an instant connection. She was a pretty good cook herself and loved to party. She seemed to get a real kick out of Malcolm. It was ironic that they liked each other, given the sexual tension between Brian and me. . . . I was always surprised they didn't suspect anything was up. Anyway, it was comfortable and fun. I found myself comparing Brian to Malcolm. I told myself to stop it.

For our second anniversary, Malcolm and I took a trip to Hawaii. I had always wanted to see the snow-white beaches, to swim in the warm turquoise water. When we arrived, we busied ourselves swimming, snorkeling, and playing tennis, and took advantage of our still-heated sexual attraction. Malcolm, who usually read nothing but cookbooks, had picked up a John Grisham novel, and would ask me about the legal points in the plot. I was happy about his interest in my field of knowledge, and it was exciting, and sexually energizing, to spend some unencumbered time with my husband again. I gave him a lot of sugar during that trip. But then, after we got home, the fire dwindled—the law firm started grinding me up, and Malcolm, as always, was immersed in his work. We went back to our "ships passing in the night" routine.

One day at work, a few months later, Brian and I were going down the elevator after an evening of legal research in the library. Out of the blue, he just grabbed me and kissed me in the elevator. It was a tongue-down-my-throat kiss, a good kiss. I didn't resist or protest; I just hugged him closer to me. I could feel my nipples stiffening against my bra, my underwear getting moist. For a moment I thought about doing it with him, right there in the elevator. But the bell rang, the elevator stopped at another floor, and a few of the cleaning crew got in. They acted oblivious to Brian and me, but with my Catholic guilt, I feared they could read my face like a book.

I figured Brian just wanted to fuck me, so the next morning I told him we should just sleep together and get it over with so we could move on in our friendship. He said he wanted to sleep with me, but it wasn't something he wanted to get over with. "There's a lot more than a friendship here, Dina," he said.

A few days later we were both supposed to be going to the officer installation of the National Conference of Black Lawyers—a boring three-hour lunch program at a big hotel downtown. When we got there, he drove right past to the next hotel. We got a room and fell into bed together. Brian didn't have Malcolm's compact, muscular build; he was long and lean. I was delighted to discover that he was a patient and attentive lover. If we could have thought of a credible excuse to tell at the firm, we would have stayed all night.

Afterward, Brian dropped me off in front of our building, and I went up the elevator while he was parking the car. I knew I was wearing the glow of love, and I didn't want anyone to see me. Luckily, my secretary was in the copy room when I walked past her desk, so I shut myself in my office. I took out the file I'd been working on that morning and opened it. But even though I was turning the pages, I wasn't absorbing anything. I was so confused, so conflicted, that I just couldn't work. In fact, I left the office to go shoe shopping—trying on Isaac Mizrahi mules, strappy Manolo Blahnik sandals, and Via Spiga leather boots always helps me clear my thoughts. I assumed it was guilt that was eating away at me. How had a nice Catholic girl like me ended up in a love triangle like this? Was this love or just an office romance? Only time would tell.

Brian and I continued to take long lunches together and sometimes we'd go to dinner after work or drop by the local magazine stand to browse. Inevitably we would wind up at a small hotel nearby, or back at my office on my plush leather sofa. It was easy to justify the late nights to our spouses; both Janelle and Malcolm knew that our law firm required young associates to put in ridiculously long hours.

We still did stuff as a foursome on the weekends, whenever we had the time off. It might seem weird that we did things as couples, but the weirdness didn't come from hanging out together; it came from sleeping with two men I cared deeply about. I grew up thinking that my husband would be the only sexual partner I would have from the time I said "I do." But that's not how things went down for me. I loved being married, but I also loved having a lover—Brian was completely woven into the fabric of my daily life.

Sex with Brian was very different from sex with Malcolm. There's always stuff at home that gets in the way of pure rapture—piles of laundry staring you down, the unkempt yard looming large. Malcolm and I had never gotten around to the homesteading stage, so the place looked like a crash pad for both of us. Brian and I always shared the pristine privacy of a hotel suite—no muss, no fuss. It was all fun.

Malcolm never seemed to catch on that I was being unfaithful. If I'd had sex with Brian on a given day I'd put extra effort into my lovemaking with Malcolm so as not to arouse suspicion. Sometimes, my excitement from a nooner with Brian made sex with Malcolm better.

Eventually my guilt got the better of me. One Sunday morning I invited Malcolm to church. He was shocked, since we hadn't gone in years. He took a pass—I'd expected as much—so I went straight to confession. I'll never forget the way it went down.

"Bless me, Father, for I have sinned. It's been almost three years since my last confession." *Oh God, what am I doing here? How can I tell him—a priest—what I've done? How can I confess breaking my marriage vows, betraying my husband, having an affair with another man?*

"Go on, my daughter," I heard through the darkened screen. I could hear, from the hint of an Irish accent, that it was Father Reilly. Could he tell who I was from my voice? He had, after all, married us.

"I . . . um . . . I lied to my husband," I finally stammered, nervous as a little kid.

"What did you tell him?"

Think—think quick! "I . . . I told him I had to stay late at the office, on a conference call, and . . . and . . . then . . . I went out drinking with my girlfriends."

"Do you have any other sins to confess?"

"No, not really," I lied. What was I doing here? In that moment I realized that what was bothering me was not that I had cheated on my husband, but that I wasn't really sorry for doing it, and that I had no intention of stopping. I asked myself what good was confession, anyway, if you didn't really regret what you'd done? I lied again: "For this and all my other sins, I am truly sorry."

I left the church and called Brian to say I was going to the office. He was waiting for me, sitting in my big chair in front of the window. "You smell like church," he said. He was a Catholic, too. He pulled me into his lap and took my face in his hands.

So much for repentance.

Malcolm, of course, was never bothered by my late nights. One of us was always coming home later than the other. I think he figured I was just getting in the groove of working really hard to build up a nest egg for our future. I was earning more money, which took the pressure off Malcolm and allowed him to pursue his own course without hassling over the finances.

He was planning to move up to an executive chef position, and he still wanted a restaurant of his own—so he had plenty to keep him busy, too. The home life we shared was increasingly sporadic, but not unhappy. He was still fun in bed, and always had some little treat from the kitchen for me—though these interludes were less and less frequent. Things worked that way for a long time, probably because everyone's needs were being met. I guess I'm proof that you can love two different people at the same time in different ways.

You can imagine how hard it was to focus on my work. I acted a lot busier than I really was, and in general I avoided everyone except Brian. I started to feel I was living a lie. Then one day Brian came into my office and closed the door. "I love you, Dina. I never thought something like this would happen to me, but it has, and I can't help it. I want to spend the rest of my life with you. I want you to leave Malcolm. I'm pretty sure you feel as connected to me as I do to you. This must be terribly confusing. But I am here for you."

*I guess I'm proof that you can love two
different people at the same time in different ways.*

I just sat and stared at him in disbelief. He came around behind my chair and put his arms around me. After a few minutes, he asked if he should leave, and I nodded "yes."

He was right; I was confused. I really did love Brian. I wanted to be with him. But I also loved Malcolm. I wasn't ready to make a decision. He didn't press me on it for six months.

When he asked me again if I was ready to leave Malcolm, I said that I wasn't. So we carried on just as we had been doing—late-night trysts in the office, conferences at hotels—for about four more years. Things didn't end in any sort of abrupt way—they just went flat, the way a bottle of champagne does if you don't drink it right away.

4.

The Fountain of Youth

The Story of Marin Wadsworth

*M*arin responded to an e-mail I circulated. When she called, she spiced her side of the conversation with sexual references. Our face-to-face meeting confirmed my first impression—that seduction was central to all of her relationships.

None of the places I suggested to meet interested her. Instead, she arranged for us to meet on a cruise ship that had docked in a nearby harbor town. When I arrived she was already seated at a table overlooking the ocean, with an open bottle of Riesling in an ice bucket within easy reach. Her auburn hair was long, cut blunt below her lovely shoulders, which showed to advantage over her loose green boatneck top. A gorgeous riot of freckles dotted her otherwise pale skin. It was easy to imagine her as the object of many a man's desire.

Clearly, Marin was up to something, but I couldn't figure out what. When pressed, she admitted that she wanted to *seduce me with the exquisite scenery and the intense, fruity wine, just as she had been seduced by the first man who had swept her off her feet.*

Before I could get a word in edgewise, she peppered me with questions: Would I be able to capture on paper the sense of romance, privacy, and charm that surrounded her first affair? Could I sympathize with her desire to merge two lifestyles, one sanctioned, one illicit? Had I ever had an affair? I gently reminded her that I needed to be the one asking the questions.

The sweetness of the wine was part of the process, Marin said, as was the blue cheese and seared foie gras she subsequently ordered. She wanted me to experience the seduction as she had, so I would understand that for her, balance was achieved through both gastronomic and sexual satisfaction. During our leisurely interview, her big hoop earrings flashed, her eyes twinkled, and she spoke about her affairs with the saucy, salty sparkle of a buccaneer.

I'M SURE when I'm done telling you my story you're going to think I'm a slut. This bothers me because my impulses are the same as a man's; while we exalt him for flexing his muscle, we condemn a woman who is overtly sexual. It's just not okay for us to sleep around—before, during, or after marriage. I don't accept that. I believe in love, but I don't think it has to be exclusive; you just have to be sure you protect the feelings of those you love. Unfortunately, I hurt my husband, and for that I will always feel bad.

Before we got married I was totally in love with Jake, totally and completely in love with him. It wasn't just a physical attraction, although he was tall and fit from years of swimming and tennis. All the outdoor sports left him perennially tanned, but he wasn't a vacuous jock—he had an extraordinary sense of humor and was at heart an intellectual. I'll admit I was attracted to his piercing brown eyes that turned down just a bit at the corner, giving him that "come close and pet me" look. What got me right away was his sense of adventure, his willingness to try anything. I'm like that myself.

We were college sweethearts, we got married, we were footloose and fancy-free. Sex was incredible—the breadth of Jake's shoulders, the rock-hardness of his athlete's body, and his devotion to me made me ache for him. Especially when he would take business trips that would require him to be away for weeks at a time. It didn't get easier; each time I'd miss him terribly, but it goes with the territory when you get involved with someone in investment banking. Clients often come first.

A few years passed and my parents wanted to take Jake and me on a cruise along the Italian Riviera. Jake was away working with a client, so I accepted their invitation and went solo. At dinner each night everyone was given a card to fill out with the names of people we wanted to dance with. One night the table captain handed me a card with my name at the top and "Herr Klaus Lorenz" on every single line—Herr Lorenz had taken the liberty of filling out my dance card. I recognized the name as the general manager of the cruise ship. I looked over at him and thought, *Oh, no!* At first glance, I found Herr Lorenz homely and fat, no one that I would ever want to dance with.

But I was sitting with my parents and didn't want to embarrass them by being unkind to Herr Lorenz. My mother said, "You'd better level with him about your marital status." She's a smart old gal who knows where it's at. I marched right over and said, "I'm very flattered, but I'm married and I don't particularly like to dance; perhaps we could have a drink instead." He invited me to meet him later that evening.

Over a bottle of Riesling and a plate of Stilton and seared foie gras, Klaus regaled me with stories of his life at sea. He had charm and wit, and wasn't above a choice tidbit of international gossip, which intrigued me. Only from reading magazines and from watching television did I know all the film people and musicians that he seemed on familiar terms with.

Some of Klaus's engaging stories featured himself as the star, but his self-deprecating humor kept him from sounding arrogant. Around midnight, he walked me back to my cabin and kissed my hand. I closed the door after saying good night and found myself thinking, *Wow, I went from thinking the guy was fat and unattractive to being totally charmed by him.* He had an aristocratic Austrian accent and he smoked cigars, which made him seem very manly. Jake, in contrast, seemed like a neophyte.

Klaus and I spent several nights enjoying each other's company during the cruise. On the last night, he came back to my cabin to listen to some music. With Erik Satie's "Velvet Gentleman" playing softly, Klaus kissed me, and our flirting turned to fondling. But, oh dear, sex was out of the question because I virtuously (or foolishly) hadn't brought my diaphragm. Klaus offered to go get condoms but I didn't want to believe we were headed toward having sex. We kissed some more. He smelled delicious, and he watched everything I did—that was a turn-on in itself. I took pleasure in initiating our undressing, and in the sensation of exploring this new territory, his exquisite understated clothing—fine cotton, linen, silk. He did the same to me, kissing me delicately after removing each item of my clothing. It was the most agonizing, slow, deliberate strip I had ever done.

Finally, I was standing naked before him. He was seated on my divan, in only a pair of shorts, looking like an elegant pasha. A cool breeze wafted through the porthole. He noticed my goose bumps, and threw his shirt over me like a mantle. I knelt as if to be knighted, put my head in his lap, and paid him homage with my lips and tongue. Then he gently pushed me back on the sofa and gave me all the pleasure I could stand with his tongue and his fingers.

We spent another night in similar fashion. His knowledge of all these pleasures, his expertise, and his charming humor so excited me that I hated to see the trip end. At disembarkation, he kissed my hand and pressed into it his card, engraved with a family crest. I said, "I hope this isn't the only time we will ever meet." He teased, "My dear, this is just the beginning." I hoped what he said was true.

Back home, I found myself making dinner reservations with Jake at beachfront restaurants so that I could look at the ocean and feel connected to Klaus. Jake and I would drink wine together and then go home and make love, but my own passion was fueled by fantasies of dear, sturdy Klaus and his refined sense of pleasure.

One day I got a note in the mail from Klaus saying he would be in town for a meeting the following weekend. I rearranged all my plans so I could meet up with him—and this time I was prepared. In his beautiful hotel room with fresh linens and filled with flowers, champagne and caviar on the room-service cart, we picked up where we had left off. I was shaking with eagerness as I reached to undo his tie; his eyes twinkled, and he said, "No, my lovely, not so fast! The best pleasures of life should be savored." He took my hands and placed them on his shoulders; then he undressed me slowly, button by button, planting a kiss, as before, in the place of every garment he took off. I was moaning, laughing, screaming with this degree of tease! Finally we moved onto the bed. I couldn't believe he would make me wait even more, but he licked and nibbled me slowly, deliberately, and then had me do the same to him. When, finally, he let me pull him into me, I slammed into a roaring orgasm that exploded like reef surf. We found our rhythm together, and it was so intense, probably because we knew we had a limited time together. I cried in the taxi when I left, thinking, *Is this the man I'm supposed to be with?* How easy it is to confuse incredible sexual passion with love! It wasn't love, but I didn't know it then.

It's unsettling when you're so attracted to somebody. Many times I've asked myself what the difference is between lust and love. I still don't have the answer. I think your husband should nourish your body and your soul, but Jake really couldn't do that because he was so obsessed with his career. And his travel schedule was hard on both of us. In spite of this, I still liked being married to him because he was basically a good man, a decent human being, sweet. . . . I couldn't let go of the idea of us together, as a family, settling down, having kids. I'd do anything for him, and he'd do anything for me. What I got from Klaus was attention and affection. He turned out to be a symbol of what I was searching for.

> *Many times I've asked myself what the difference is between lust and love.*

Klaus, in fact, was the first in a string of affairs—and the catalyst for my next relationship, with a man named Timothy who is still a friend of mine. We met at the gym. I was working out with free weights, and he was one of the regulars—not a bodybuilder type, but just a good-looking man staying in shape. At the time, he was married to a celebrity and wasn't getting enough attention from her. Her career was outstripping his, and he felt she was blowing him off—not exactly like Jake and me, but there was a parallel. I loved sleeping with Timothy; he was totally different from Klaus. In fact, I sometimes think that every relationship is a reaction to the one before. Where Klaus was refined and polished—monogrammed silks and linens—Timothy was sweat pants and running gear. I'd just pull the string of his waistband, and we'd instantly go into action. There's something to be said for aerobics! He wasn't a patient lover; he'd press up against me in the gym and let me feel his erection. Nine times out of ten we'd be out of there before even finishing our workout, doing the wild thing in any way or place he could contrive: in the back of his SUV; in the hallway of my apartment, sitting on a window ledge behind a potted palm with my legs around his neck; on a quiet jogging path in the park, after I flung him down onto the grass; once, even, in the men's locker room, where he hauled me when I wouldn't let go of the string to his sweats, with him sitting on a wooden bench facing the mirror while we went at it. Talk about sweat! Our relationship was just about sex—with a certain amount of fitness thrown in. It continued for several months, but it wasn't exclusive for either of us. We were just—not that I like the expression— fuck buddies.

I'm reluctant to admit that at the same time I was also fooling around with a well-known actor and with the contractor on my house. None of these men was significant, to me, anyway, but that's probably because at that time, no man would have been able to satisfy all of my needs.

I wondered what Klaus would think of all my activity. In a moment of nostalgia, I called him. He laughed, and wanted to know all the details. I could talk to him like I talked to my mother! He was great. He said he was afraid it sounded as if I hadn't met my match yet, but thought it was a good thing to experience a wide variety of pleasures. He said that was what he always did. He told me that I was among his finest, and that he would always treasure our time together. Then he said that if I ever needed anything—money, plane tickets, a case of champagne—I was to call him first. That was when it clicked for me that we were really far off in our separate worlds, and that I should count him as a friend and nothing more. I'd still love to see him again.

I don't think I knew what my needs were at that point. I only know that I wanted to stay married to Jake because he was the most appropriate partner of all the men I'd been with. Unfortunately, he started to suspect that something was up and confronted me several times.

I denied everything until Jake read an e-mail I'd written to my college roommate detailing my sexual escapades. He wouldn't have seen it, but I ran out and left it on my desk after getting an urgent call to cover the register at my family's restaurant when the cashier fainted. Jake was undone by my deceit, which made me feel terrible. He moved out immediately.

I missed Jake every single day and every single night. Even though I'd been sleeping with other men, I loved Jake and I believed he loved me. Until the day he left we were having regular sex, married sex that wasn't particularly exciting because it was so predictable. Jake and I failed because I wasn't ready to settle down, and because he traveled so much for business. I learned that love alone isn't enough to sustain a marriage. I wanted to get remarried—to try again. I met my second husband ten months after Jake and I split up. Our best date was our first date. After the second margarita, Don turned to me and said, "God, I think I love you. . . . Is it possible to fall in love at first sight? The truth is, I do love you, and I want to spend the night with you."

I learned that love alone isn't enough to sustain a marriage.

I didn't love Don that night, but I was attracted to him—and I was certainly interested in the sleeping together part! He seemed likable, too. He was a little older than me. He had been seriously involved with a woman for several years, but that didn't work out; she hadn't wanted to have children, and they drifted apart. He had dated a little but hadn't found anyone who'd seriously interested him—until he saw me. We spent six months together and then he said he wouldn't see me any more until my divorce from Jake was final. So I got my divorce—a summary dissolution, which was way too easy. I don't think I took enough time to process what had happened to us. I do know our divorce was my fault because I had been sleeping with other men.

I wanted to be open with Don about all this, so I just told him the truth. He's a lawyer, so he cross-examined me, you might say, about the whole history of my marriage and my affairs. He listened impartially, like a judge.

About Klaus, he said, "He sounds like a great guy! I'd like to meet him!" About Timothy, he raised an eyebrow and said, "I know who he is. That guy gets around." Still, he reserved judgment. All he said was, "It's good to know what you don't like while you're finding what you do like." I was looking for three things when I married Don. I wanted children, I wanted a house, and I wanted someone I could talk to. Don said he would give me all that and more. So we got married and I let go of my regrets about Jake.

Some years passed. Don and I had two children, and were comfortable in our marriage. I was finally able to make peace with myself for messing up my first marriage. I was still attracted to other men, but I didn't allow myself to entertain thoughts of straying, choosing, instead, to focus on our young sons. Until the inevitable happened.

We were at a fundraiser and there was this cute guy standing next to me in the dessert buffet line. The woman serving asked me what kind of ice cream I wanted. "Banana nut," I said. The cute guy looked at me and laughed; never did I hear such provocative innuendo in a laugh. We had a brief flirty chat before I went back to my seat. Don and I left the party right after dessert and I forgot all about the other guy.

A month later we were at a dinner party and I noticed the man from the ice cream line chatting with some people across the room.

My heart started beating faster and then he looked over at me. He didn't smile, and he didn't take his eyes off me. Dinner was announced and everyone moved toward the table. Suddenly this man was standing next to me and pulling out my chair. I looked around for Don, who was in the next room, laughing with the host. It became apparent that couples weren't sitting together, so I sat down in the proffered chair and turned to my right. "I'm Martin," he said, before I had the chance to introduce myself.

Martin and I engaged in light banter during the salad course. He pointed out his wife, an attractive redhead seated at the other end of the table. *Fair enough, I've been warned*, I thought. We talked about his work. And then, during the main course, I felt his leg pressing against mine under the table. At first I thought it was accidental. But when he didn't move it, I realized he intended it to be there and it would be up to me to move my leg away. I didn't. I pressed back. I was trying to keep my breathing shallow but it was hard. I took a big swig of pouilly-fuissé, and then spent the rest of the meal wondering if anyone could tell how excited I was.

I don't know how he got my cell phone number, but the next day he called and asked me if I wanted to get together. He didn't say anything sexually explicit but I knew from his vibe that this was going to be about sex. After Klaus, this guy's approach wasn't particularly classy, but, in hindsight, I think it was the only way he knew.

During that phone call, Martin told me he was unhappily married and had been having an affair with his personal assistant. She'd recently become engaged and had cut off things cold turkey, which left Martin feeling lonely and out of sorts. He made it clear that he didn't want to leave his wife because they had young children, but he told me he wasn't in love with her. I'm not sure what it was about Martin that appealed to me, but underneath his bravado was an irresistible vulnerability.

Don and I were getting along quite well, although sex with the same person does get monotonous. The thought of having a no-strings-attached affair was intriguing. I suggested meeting Martin the next afternoon in the parking lot of the local mall. I got into his car and I confessed to him that I'd had sex with my husband the night before but had fantasized that it was Martin. He grinned and said, "I'm glad you said that," and leaned over to kiss me. We fooled around for a long time in the car but I wasn't willing to have intercourse because I didn't know who he had been with. I just couldn't go there now that I had children. I didn't want to take any chances.

He suggested we get a hotel room but I said, "We're not going to a hotel. We're going to go upstairs and we're going to eat." We went to an Indian restaurant and shared a sumptuous, exotic meal. He lightly, playfully caressed my face, my hands, my thighs as we dined and chatted. We talked about movies and music—and then we went back to our separate cars and said good night. Needless to say, my husband got the benefit of all my arousal that night.

Martin called me the next morning and asked me to meet him again. I said, "I don't want to do this! You're going through a midlife crisis, and that's not my problem. I've been there; I understand it but I'm not going to do it again." He accepted my position, didn't fight me on it, didn't appear to be upset, and didn't call me back. I was bumming at that, because the day before it had seemed like he couldn't live without me. I can't explain why, but I felt angst about him for a year.

And then we were both invited back to the home of our mutual friends. I was newly pregnant with my second child at the time, but I looked at Martin and I wanted him. He was cerebral, on the fringe of the entertainment industry, but not so sucked in that all he cared about was "making it." Yet he was introspective, really smart—and heavily cool. Somehow he looked handsomer than before—more confident, more buff, more together. I looked at him, and all I could think about was sleeping with him. But he showed no interest. I learned that night that Martin had separated from his wife and was renting a house close by. He steered clear of me.

A few years later, Don and I took the kids to Mexico and in an unusual twist of fate, wound up at the same hotel that Martin was in with his kids. I hadn't seen him since the night he'd been so aloof, and I was totally surprised to run into him by the pool one afternoon. I mustered my courage and said, "I'm sorry

I was rude the last time we spoke. The truth is, I would like to be with you." He said, "It's not possible, not now." I think he saw the look of disappointment on my face. "You're married," he said, "so you're not available. I don't want to do that to you, or to me." I was upset—devastated, actually; but I didn't want him to know. I shrugged, and said, "Well, it was worth a try!" and we parted on friendly terms. But I thought, *I will find somebody who wants me. I will.*

I didn't get how he could not want me! I'm beautiful, I'm smart, I'm funny, and I wanted him. What guy is going to walk away from that? I didn't realize that there are a lot of smart, beautiful, available single women he could be with. There was one other factor; when he was married he wanted to sleep with me, but once he was single he wanted a woman who was available. It makes perfect sense to me now.

That night I went to a pay phone and called my mother. I'll never forget her reaction. In her total savviness, she said, "Darling, you're going to have to find somebody else who's in your same pickle, if that's what you feel you need to do. You have to find someone else who's married."

My mother was right. Six months later I met a man in the lobby bar of the Bellagio Hotel in Las Vegas. I was in town for a cousin's funeral; Robert was there on business. We wound up having dinner that night and he told me that although he was attracted to me, he was deeply religious and wouldn't allow himself to have sex with anyone other than his wife. *Oh, boy, here's a fine fish,* I thought. Still stinging from Martin's rejection, I was determined to have him to restore my own sense of equilibrium. I lured him to my room by telling him that my view of the dancing fountains was better than his—a "must-see."

Inside the room, I opened a bottle of Belvedere vodka from the minibar and poured him a drink. Then I smiled at him and lay down on the bed, motioning for him to join me. He was clearly conflicted, because he stayed on the other side of the bed for a while before I pulled him over to me.

Robert didn't want to spend the night; he said he was worried his wife would call. I didn't care. I needed to have sex with him to reassure myself that I still had it—and thankfully, I did. He scurried back to his room right afterward, probably to call his wife. Turned out to be the kind of fish you throw back right after you catch him.

When I got back from that trip, I arranged for my kids to stay with friends. I asked Don to meet me upstairs at 8:30 and then spent many hours making up for my secret sins. I think he assumed the funeral was depressing so I came home needing a release.

Sometimes I wonder if I should be straight with my husband about my attraction to other men—my little escapades. He knows my history better than anyone. Could he think that I wouldn't change? My past didn't bother him when we first met; he seemed amused by it. I'm sometimes tempted to tell him, "Oh, I find so-and-so attractive" or "I met someone today who had me thinking naughty thoughts." I don't know—would he freak out, like Jake did, and terminate the marriage? Or would he find it intriguing? I've read that some men are aroused by the thought of their women with other men.

I guess I have to play this one by ear.

The way I see it, I've only got a few more years before I'm too old to be desirable to anyone, even my husband. In the meantime I say, "Carpe diem."

5.

Foreign Affairs

The Story of Chantal Dickerson

*C*hantal and I were introduced by a mutual colleague. She lived in a grand old American Colonial house, complete with a little fountain burbling in the green courtyard beneath an ancient, white-limbed sycamore, and a view of the bay. The impression I had was not just of wealth, but of security and history—a solid American foundation.

Chantal had invited me to her home because her family was gone for the day. She felt comfortable having me over because we had been introduced by a client of mine who she also did work for. The surprise inside her home was the color. Not the floors, which were light parquet and marble; not the walls, which were neutral; but the fabrics and the furniture, the paintings and the simple decorations, which were a shock of hot pink, lime green, turquoise, and tangerine—chosen for simplicity of line, and arranged by someone who loved surprises and knew what she was doing. It was Chantal who had chosen this palette of delight. A painter herself, she had an unerring sense of how to mix the mod and the trad. When I commented on the beauty of her plan of contrasts, she grinned and pulled aside a long, silvery velvet curtain that shaded the drawing room from the western sun. It was lined in fuchsia silk.

Chantal herself was a study in fusion. She wasn't quite tall, and she wasn't quite thin; she was curvy, like a concubine, with wavy dark hair and light hazel eyes. She was dressed in classic colors, with a nod to the fifties—pale gray capri pants, ballerina flats, a white scoopneck jersey—but had included what I call one of her startling colors—a hot-pink headband.

Her father was French, she said, and her mother a "generic Anglo-American." She had a huge extended family, and they played a large role in her life. The wealth came to her from her husband, a principal in a large investment bank. She'd studied art and had hoped to travel, but that dream was sidelined by her early marriage. She still took classes occasionally, but she had developed as a painter on her own—her diligent work habits supported by a large and lively household staff. Her passions were her two children and her studio, which she showed me on the way to the veranda where we had tea. The art room was a jumble of color and artifacts, with stacks of paintings leaning nonchalantly against the walls, a contrast to the deliberate arrangement of the rest of the house. She grinned. "This is the only door I keep shut."

We went out to the shady balcony for tea, and as she talked, she dangled a shoe off one foot and gestured with her arms and hands.

MY HUSBAND wasn't the most attractive or the most interesting man I had ever met, but he was the steadiest. And he was very kind. I decided very early on that I needed to choose between passion and security in a husband, because I couldn't have both. I knew if I married John, I'd have a great life, a great family, and complete security. That was supposed to compensate for the lack of passion.

> *I decided very early on that I needed to choose between passion and security in a husband, because I couldn't have both.*

I had decided to marry John because I knew he would be a good provider and father. Before him, I had always fallen in love with the wrong kind of guy—the guy who would wine and dine you and then break your heart. My love life could be described as a parade of the jerks. I was attracted to the bad boys, the outlaws, the renegades.

Walking down the aisle, I felt both happy and sad, knowing I was giving up on the ideal of true passion but at the same time getting someone who would be around for the long haul. I wasn't going to have the highs, but I also wasn't going to have the lows. Security was also something to be desired, something I hadn't had before.

Nature abhors a vacuum. If you stop talking, someone will fill the silence. I didn't have passion in my marriage, but I accepted that, at first. I had my children to raise. To make our sex life better, I gave myself permission to fantasize in order to create the passion that was missing. When I made love to my husband, I thought about someone else. Usually, I picked a minor movie star, someone over the hill, like Timothy Dalton. Someone who, if circumstances presented, I might possibly meet. Fantasizing about someone like Brad Pitt, whom I could never be with, wouldn't work. It could be someone I randomly met, or someone I worked with. The cast of characters was always changing.

At one point, I latched on to a fantasy involving a man I met at the gym. He was perfect—tall, dark, handsome, and Italian. I've always been attracted to foreign men; it is odd that I married someone who's so Jack Kennedy. I lusted after this guy for weeks—all in my mind, because we'd never even spoken—until one day, out of the blue, he came over to me and introduced himself. And then he invited me to go have a Jamba Juice with him after our workout. His name was Mario.

Getting to know him intensified my attraction. My desire for him felt like a tidal wave that couldn't be contained. He didn't hit on me, but we developed a friendship. We saw each other once or twice a week, almost always at the gym. In retrospect it was emotional foreplay. This went on for two years. He was very attractive, but the real intimacy was in the conversations we had. At first he didn't say he wanted to sleep with me, but when he finally did, I told him the feeling was mutual.

Mario was worldly; he'd been to more places than I've ever dreamed about and he spoke at least five languages. He was planning to settle down not far from where I lived. I knew my desire for him was selfish, but he was so much more interesting to me than my husband. I was turned on by his lively intelligence. He expressed himself easily, and well. He was beautiful. He had a beautiful voice, beautiful hands. I sketched him over and over, from memory, when we were apart.

He kissed me for the first time when I was pregnant with my second child. I was about five months along, and feeling terrific; I wasn't huge, just starting to show. My lips were fuller, my breasts bigger, and I felt full of the hormones of plenty. I loved pregnancy, and both John and I were eager for another baby. Mario and I were out for coffee one day and he was sitting next to me, touching my arm lightly, almost protectively—he was so gallant, and seemed to cherish my maternal state. Then he held my hand and, almost like a slow dance move, he pulled me up from my chair at the same time that he stood up. We were so close and then he was lifting up my chin with his hand. He kissed me, on my face, my brow, my lips.

It felt very comfortable but it was also very romantic—no tongue-action, just beautiful, somehow in keeping with the richly sensual, yet chaste, coffee date we were having.

As we were getting up to leave, he took hold of me and asked, "So, are you feeling okay with things?" meaning the kiss. He was truly concerned. I told him it had been a very long time since I had felt that kind of passion. I enjoyed myself so much that day. I still think of him whenever I go to that coffee house.

Later that afternoon, he called me and said we had to meet the following morning; it was important. I said that would be fine.

The next morning, right after I dropped my son at school, I drove straight to the parking lot of the gym. He was already there, waiting for me. He walked up to my car and told me he was deeply in love with me.

It was an incredible moment for me, the acknowledgment of what I'd been feeling. When I told him the feeling was mutual, it felt as if we had established a kind of truce. Shortly after that, my doctor said that I had to stay in bed if I wanted to continue the pregnancy. It was almost a relief; I couldn't do anything. I arranged everything I needed close at hand—books, sketchbooks, crayons, magazines, the telephone. I talked with Mario every day on the phone about what we were doing each day, about the news, about things we were interested in, about our longing for one another. We had endless things to talk about.

Then I had the baby, and she was wonderful, but a baby takes all your attention and puts quite a damper on outside things. Still, I was back at the gym as soon as the doctor said it was safe, which, for me, was pretty quick. Mario and I saw each other often; we just didn't consummate anything.

Even during that time, he looked at me as if he desired me. Whenever he would touch me, I felt great. Some people have a good touch. There was never any magic when my husband touched me. When I slept with my husband—usually about once a week, and always because he wanted to—he was sweet and loving, but I always had to psych myself up with a few glasses of wine and a good fantasy.

One evening when my husband was working late, I dropped by Mario's place to visit. He was lifting weights and looking sexy and sweaty. I dropped my coat to reveal a lace g-string. I'd been going to the gym regularly and I was feeling pretty good, especially for a woman who'd recently had a baby. And I was ready to resume my adult life.

I said, "Do you want to make love to me?"

He said, "Yes."

So he did.

Mario was incredible. The three years of buildup created tremendous anticipation on both sides. We had been intimate on so many levels, in so many ways. Finally, we achieved the physical confirmation of our longing. I wondered if I could ever again get by on fantasy alone.

Mario said it was like a bell that you cannot un-ring. Once it's done, it's done. He took it very seriously. It wasn't as if he just wanted to have his way and run off.

That first night we consummated our relationship to the fullest; then I got dressed and went home to cook dinner for my family. Once everyone was fed, I supervised the children's homework. I was very happy.

After the second or third time Mario and I made love, I was lying in his arms when he said to me, "I wonder if we'll ever know what it's like to spend the whole night together." I wanted to find out as much as he did.

Meanwhile, I was living my married life—driving the kids to and from school or Mommy & Me classes; working, painting, organizing the household, and throwing dinner parties for our friends. Sometimes I would make love to Mario in the early afternoon, then go directly from his apartment to pick the kids up. There were also times when I had sex with both men on the same day, but that wasn't a problem for me. It was like two entirely different worlds I was living in. With each man, I was a different woman. Sex with Mario was about desire and passion; sex with John was about fulfilling my wifely duty. Which I always did. Once I'd met Mario, I stopped fantasizing about famous people and started thinking only of him during sex with John.

John never knew about Mario. He has too pure a soul to suspect that I was involved with another man. He would be deeply hurt if he ever knew what I was up to.

When Mario had asked me why I was with my husband, and what was lacking in my relationship, I told him the truth. Marrying John was an intellectual decision. I didn't feel the passion that had always screwed me up with men in the past, and that was a relief. He was a good man, and we did a good job of raising our two children together. Before my wedding I asked my mother if I should marry John. She said, "Love comes later. True love can grow over time if the relationship is properly nourished."

Well, she was wrong. At least in my case. If you don't have passion to start with, it's not going to happen later. It never happened.

The fact that I was having an affair did not mean there was anything different in my marriage. It didn't suddenly get worse or change, and my husband didn't become different. Loving Mario was part of what I needed to do to keep myself centered.

I still love John, in a rather platonic way. He thinks I'm the happy housewife, and I hope he always does. He's supportive, totally indulgent about my work; he's interested in, though ignorant of, art, so we talk about that a lot. It's neutral ground. I've made it my mission to make sure that my husband and my children are happy.

My relationship with Mario wasn't complicated. He wasn't demanding, but he was available and patient. There was no craziness or weirdness. He said he would wait for me for ten years, when my kids were old enough, and then he would marry me. He wanted to grow old with me.

One time, when my husband was out of town, I met Mario at a hotel near my home. We made love all night long. It was as if all the things we'd been waiting to express to each other came out through our bodies—the yearning, the tenderness, the knowledge. But the next day I was wracked with guilt about leaving my kids home with a babysitter. I waited almost a year before I did that again. It was bad enough sneaking out during the day—leaving the kids overnight was another story.

Another time I returned from a trip with my family, and went out to meet Mario for a smoothie. I hadn't seen him for a while and I said, jokingly, "I've cheated on you"—meaning I had been having sex with my husband. He was aghast; he thought I meant someone other than my husband. I thought I was being playful, but he didn't get it. He was having heart palpitations. He made it clear that if I was ever with anyone other than my husband, that would be it for us.

Another time, I was exercising with a male personal trainer and Mario said, winking at me, "If you were married to me, you would never have a male exercise instructor. I know what goes on at the gym."

I realized I couldn't engage in Mario's dreams. He assumed I was willing to live a lie for ten years and then say, "Sorry, John, we've raised our kids together, but now it's time for me to go off and spend the rest of my life with someone I've been cheating with." I did want to be with Mario—but I couldn't imagine leaving John. This was difficult to reconcile.

I broke it off a couple of times, whenever I would start to feel that I couldn't keep living the lie. I was also a tiny bit suspicious of a man who could be satisfied by the kind of relationship we were having. I kept telling him he needed to meet someone else, because this wasn't good for him. He would say he loved me, and he saw himself living out the rest of his life with me. He insisted there was no one else. I always told him, "If you need somebody, just tell me, because you will. You're single, I'm not."

I told myself he was eventually going to meet someone; it was only a matter of time. I worried about that, because I didn't want to give my heart to someone who was going to break it. That was the reason I married someone safe—to protect myself. But whenever Mario and I made love, it was incredible—a true connection: emotional, sexual, everything. We would look at each other and I would wonder what I was doing.

"I've never loved anyone like I love you," he would tell me.

When I asked him if he had been with anyone else he said, "No. I fully realize you are a married woman. I can't be with anyone else. What happens if I pass something on to you? I totally understand my responsibility, that I could never be with someone else."

But slowly I discovered that he was not being entirely up-front with me about everything. He was supposed to come see me in another city while I was there visiting a gallery, but when I arrived, he wasn't there. I was shocked and hurt. I called him and asked why he hadn't come when he'd said he would. He said he was sorry, but he had assumed I didn't want him to come. How could he leave me hanging that way? I pushed him a little, and he finally showed up.

When he arrived, I was waiting to punish him for making me grovel. I felt like I had put so much on the line, and I was the one with so much to lose. It was the first time I didn't feel we were on the same page with regard to our relationship. We had an okay time, but it wasn't nearly as good as I had imagined.

A few days after we got home, I showed up at his work. I had had trouble reaching him the night before; he told me he was at a concert with his friend, Shane, and couldn't hear his cell phone. While we were talking, Shane showed up and Mario ran out to talk to him.

I thought, *Uh oh. This is bad.*

I walked out to confront Shane, who didn't know what hit him. Mario was trying to spoon-feed him details of his lie. It was so obvious it was almost funny. The truth is, I was furious. He said he had never lied to me about anything, but he had felt put on the spot.

I started to doubt our entire relationship.

I didn't want to continue if we were just going to be some casual sex thing. What was I to Mario? I didn't have any other kind of emotional or physical outlet; Mario had become every-thing to me. He had endless hours to meet other women while

I was home being a wife and mother. I didn't want to be his safety net that he would come back to between other flings. That would not do.

Finally he invited me over to lunch. I went to his place; we had lunch; he played music; we went to bed. While we were having sex, he used the word *fucking* and said the best sex we ever had was the night we'd spent in the hotel. It was starting to sound as if all Mario cared about was the sexual part of our relationship. I didn't get it. I assumed he had met someone else.

I decided to make myself completely unavailable to him. I didn't answer my phone; I didn't return his calls—nothing. He was unable to reach me after that. He sent me a couple of letters. They were very romantic. I saved every one of them. Finally I called him to say that they were nice. I explained that things needed to change or we couldn't be together again. He didn't call for a while because he thought I was sending a signal that I wanted to break up. It was a miscommunication.

More than once he wooed me back against my better judgment. Then he called me on my birthday and told me he was moving back to Italy. I had been with him for six years, and now he was going to leave for good.

I probably hurt him by cutting him off. But I thought that if he really loved me as he said he did, he would fight for us. Maybe he wanted to get revenge on me, or stomp on my heart; or maybe he just realized I would never be available to him. The ten-year plan wasn't going to work. Of course it wasn't.

He left, and soon afterward I found out that he had a girlfriend during two years of our relationship, whom I hadn't known about. By the time this got back to me, I had no way to reach him. I wasn't able to confront him, which left things unresolved.

I distinctly remember the last time I went back to him. I was still seriously in love with him. It had been a month since we had talked, and he had not yet told me that he was moving away.

I asked him, "Since you've been with me, have you been with anybody else?"

In the middle of making love, he said, "Not even close. I love you. More than you'll ever know."

It was a lie.

Why couldn't he just have told me? We were so intimate. The physical part was minor in a way, compared to all the time we had spent talking and learning about each other, and exploring our feelings together. We were both in love. Or so I thought.

When I think about him, I just want to be with him. It wasn't all sex for me. I could lie in his arms completely content. I miss him so much.

Unfaithful, that movie, got it wrong. You could tell a man wrote and directed it. He didn't capture the language; he didn't get the attraction. The thing that got her in the first place was the fact that he could quote Omar Khayyam. He lured her with that. He was an expert; he knew more than she did about something, which fascinated her, but they didn't go with that. He was sexy, but they tried to make it seem like it was all about sex. How is that going to tempt a woman, who was obviously married to a great guy, to stray? It wasn't just the sex. It was the emotion, too.

A few weeks after Mario moved away, I got a message from him thanking me for the note I'd sent. He said he would write, but I didn't hear from him. I was crushed.

He called me once, on the anniversary of when we first met, after several months had gone by. When he called I was all bubbly and I said I was still in love with him. But on the inside, I was bitter, because he had always known I had another relationship to maintain, but I never knew that he did. It served me right—I suppose this was my punishment for cheating on John.

The bottom line in all this is that my relationship with Mario was false. We didn't wake up with each other, or go shopping together, or answer each other's phones.

I made sure that my family was happy—particularly John. I made sure I didn't get caught. In the process I lost my heart.

I often wonder if Mario will come back. I don't know the answer to that.

So?

I'm grateful that I can't contact him, because there are times I would call him and say, "I don't care. I still love you. Please come back."

Fantasy used to enable me to get through my marriage. But the stakes were so much higher with a real flesh-and-blood person. It's ironic that Mario broke my heart. I married John because he was emotionally safe. But then I got involved with someone who hurt me the way I was trying not to be hurt.

A real attraction is often an accident. Mario happened accidentally. I wasn't at a bar. I wasn't looking, and for a long time I was just imagining a relationship with him. Everything happened so slowly, which made it more intense, and therefore it wasn't resolved quickly or easily.

I have a sex drive, but what I really long for is romance, intimacy, and sharing stories with someone I feel passionate about. Becoming intimate with someone other than my husband was good for me for a long time. But once Mario disappeared from my life, it was over for him, but not for me. The memories linger in my senses; I can still smell Mario, though it's been three years since he left.

I suspect that I'll have several more affairs. I need distraction. I need passion. But I'm not out there looking. When it's meant to be, it will be.

I exercise with a handsome trainer named Tony. He looks like Liam Neeson, and we talk about food. About whether the French fries at In-N-Out Burger are better than the French fries at McDonald's. I have no interest in him, even though he's gorgeous. He would tell me to "lay down" and I would think, *It's not lay down; it's lie down, you idiot!* Those things bother me. Someone has to have a real gift for the language and be able to wrap his tongue around a word properly for me to be attracted to him.

Tony's butchering of the English language has made me appreciate my husband's command of it. But since fantasy is always better than reality, tonight when John and I are in bed, I'll close my eyes and think of Russell Crowe, rather than think of England, as Queen Victoria once suggested.

6.

A Taste for Passion

The Story of Melissa Colbert

*M*y friend Gwen told me about Melissa. "I doubt she's like any of the other women you've talked to." When I questioned her, all Gwen would say is, "You'll see for yourself when you meet her." Melissa was from Wisconsin, but she was traveling to LA for her niece's graduation. She had reservations at the Century Plaza, which is not far from where I live. I asked Gwen for her phone number so I could call her.

When we spoke that evening I conducted a sort of pre-interview—to understand her story and see how it contrasted with other stories I'd heard so far. Melissa was happy to oblige, regaling me with her sexual adventures. Her life was quite different from the lives of the others I'd spoken to, so I arranged to meet her. She was clearly a seductress, so I assumed she would exude some overt sexuality.

But when we met the next day, I was shocked by Melissa's

appearance. She was very overweight, which made it hard for me to picture her living the life she had described. Melissa launched right into her story, and while we were talking, our waiter delivered copious amounts of food to the table. Melissa explained that she had taken the liberty of ordering while she was waiting for me to arrive. As we started in on our meal, I learned quickly that food was not the only appetite Melissa liked to indulge to excess.

LL MY life I've been fighting the battle of the bulge. Controlling my impulses has always been hard for me—even as a child—but when my first marriage to a guy named Adam ended after six months, I took it pretty hard and found comfort in quarts of Dulce de Leche Häagen Dazs ice cream.

It was shocking to learn that Adam had cheated on me so soon after our wedding—we'd dated for nine years, so his deceit was totally devastating. I never saw him or spoke to him once we split. His behavior emotionally destroyed me, so it's ironic that I've gone from victim to perpetrator. There are no excuses for what I did.

I was overweight when I met my second husband, Lyle, and he fell in love with me despite my size. After Adam, I was looking for someone I could trust. Lyle's not particularly attractive, but he's a very nice man and I was drawn to his kindness. We had a lovely, simple wedding at our local church with a reception in a nearby hotel. Lyle was a virgin when we got married because he wanted to "wait until he was in love." There was something hopelessly romantic about him saving himself and it served as a narcissistic yet effective aphrodisiac for the first few years of our marriage. I really got off on the notion that I was his "one and only." Lyle swore he would never cheat on me and I believed him. It didn't matter to him how much I weighed.

On our honeymoon I got pregnant with our first son. My eating was out of control during my pregnancy, and I wasn't able to lose much weight after giving birth.

Huge doesn't begin to describe how I looked after my second child was born a few years later. Luckily, Lyle never gave me any grief about it. He obviously loved me. It was ironic, since I didn't love myself. Even when the doctor put me on the scale and said I weighed 260 pounds, it didn't seem possible that my weight had gotten so out of control. "Your scale's wrong," I said to him. If only it were so. He prescribed Fen-Phen and sent me home with a diet and exercise plan. For the first time ever, I embraced the idea of losing weight as if my life depended on it.

On my new Fen-Phen diet, the weight came off, and a new woman emerged. Though the pills had helped me shed a few pounds, the real transformation came after I'd been in bed with a really bad stomach flu. Unable to eat, I lost ten pounds without feeling deprived. A week later, feeling slimmer and sexier, I took myself shopping. For the first time in years I bought clothing that showed off my figure. Goodbye shy, overweight housewife, hello extroverted sex kitten! The actual beginning of my new life started when a handsome auditor came into my office needing some documents. Feeling attractive and confident in my new persona, I laughed and flirted with this guy in a way that was totally new for me. What should have been a brief conversation lasted for about an hour. I don't remember any of it because all I could think about while we were talking was, *Wow, he's great looking.* So distracting was the conversation that afterward I had to ask my assistant what his name was. Jimmy Webber—a beautiful name for a beautiful man. And it wasn't just his looks. He smelled as if he'd just stepped out of the shower, and his graying stubble was really sexy.

Having an interoffice crush really helped me with the weight loss. I'd look at a cookie and tell myself not to eat it—that Jimmy might stop flirting with me if I gained weight. It became easier and easier to give up the junk. A month passed and during that time, Jimmy called my office a few times for this and that while he was traveling, and we flirted over the phone.

One day Jimmy finally asked me if I wanted to have lunch. We went for sushi and sake. That lunch was the first of many—after that, we made a habit of grabbing lunch at mostly quick, casual restaurants within walking distance of our office. Jimmy wasn't married, but he knew I was. It didn't seem to be a problem for him, though; he never even mentioned it.

About a month later, Jimmy made a reservation for us at a fancy French bistro. While we were waiting for our appetizer to arrive, he leaned over the table and said, "I'm very attracted to you." Shocked, nervous, and excited, I didn't know what to say. I blurted out, "I could never . . ." and then let my words fade out unconvincingly. To his credit, Jimmy took the rejection in stride. He didn't press the point or argue. What a gentleman he was.

Over the next month, Jimmy called, visited my office, and took me to lunch like nothing had happened. Then, about five or six weeks after he made his first stab, he took a second try. "I really meant it when I said I was attracted to you," he said, piercing me with his deep brown eyes. This time I responded, saying the feeling was mutual. It sounds corny, but we really did sit there staring into each other's eyes. Both of us seemed paralyzed by the exchange. "Do you want to do anything about it?" he asked. "Maybe," I said, tempted.

Making love with Lyle that night, I could only think of Jimmy and what it would be like to sleep with him. If he was half as good as I fantasized he would be, I was in for a big surprise.

The very next day Jimmy and I agreed to act upon our shared attraction. Even though I had no reason to betray my husband, I felt that I could keep both relationships separate. As long as I kept my husband sexually satisfied and was a good mother to my children, did it really matter? One relationship had nothing to do with the other, so I agreed to meet him at a hotel.

I will forever remember the image of Jimmy lying comfortably in nothing but his skin, sprawled across a tightly made bed in that beautiful body, beckoning me to him as I sat across the room, shaking in my polyester office clothes, day-old nylons, and cellulite-ridden dimpled skin. I was genuinely scared and wondered what the hell I was doing there. Deep down, I wanted to conquer my fears, as if sleeping with this man would put the fat housewife that had taken over my self-esteem permanently out of her misery.

"You're nervous aren't you, baby? Come here. Lie down next to me," was the first and last thing I remember him saying to me.

That evening was unlike anything I'd ever experienced before. Jimmy was wild, doing things to and with my body that I'd never imagined. He handled me like a master craftsman and I responded as if I had never been touched before.

My husband and Jimmy were polar opposites in every imaginable way. The only thing they had in common was me. Jimmy was big and buff, Lyle small. Jimmy had model good looks. My husband simply did not. Jimmy was a *bon vivant* who'd left hundreds of satisfied women in his wake. My husband had only been with me. As I surrendered to the unexpected pleasure Jimmy introduced me to, it became less and less clear to me why having only one lover in your life is supposed to be a good thing.

It became less and less clear to me why having only one lover in your life is supposed to be a good thing.

I rationalized my actions by telling myself that I was making up for lost time. After devoting myself to my first husband for nine years, he shit on me. Unfortunately, Lyle had to pay for the mistakes that my first husband made. I was a fat girl who never had a lot of choices, so when Jimmy came along, I felt entitled. This was a once-in-a-lifetime opportunity—to be with someone really desirable—that I wasn't going to pass up. My motto was simple: "Don't get caught."

I worked in sales, and since I traveled a lot for business, it was easy for Jimmy and me to be together. For almost three years, we had the most amazing sex together. He was innovative, penetrating every orifice in my body. Over and over and over. For the first time in my life, something other than food was fueling me.

The only guilt I had was about Lyle. My husband never did anything wrong, and he didn't deserve to have a cheating wife. He gave me plenty of attention at home, but that didn't stop me from carrying on with Jimmy. There's no way to deny that I was enthusiastically living a double life. It was as if I was single when I was with Jimmy. In time, the lines between my diverging worlds became so blurred that I lost my sense of boundaries and invited Jimmy to my home for a Christmas party and then again for a Super Bowl party. This is one of my biggest regrets; it was wrong to put my husband and my lover in the same room together. But these occasions, which had always been food orgies for me in the past, turned into wonderful weight-loss days. The anticipation of Jimmy's caresses made it easy for me to resist food.

For the first time in my life, I was thin. I was working out every day and finally reached my goal of size eight. I looked hot and I liked looking hot. My husband and my boyfriend also liked that I looked hot, and soon other men began to notice, too. Getting attention for the way I looked was a new and truly exciting experience. I'd spent my life on the outside of "the thin life," pounding at the window to get in. Sleeping with Jimmy made me feel accepted, as if I was on the inside. My heightened self-esteem led me further away from the fat girl I once was to the sex kitten I became.

I thought I was being a good mother during this time. My pediatrician had always said, "Happy mommy, happy baby." It made sense to me. I was in great spirits, satiated by the great sex. It's a good thing my boys were too young to notice my comings and goings. We had a great nanny who carted them to and from school and their various activities, so their needs were being met.

It didn't help that everyone thought Jimmy was "such a nice guy." And he was. He always told me to stay married; he said I had a great life, great kids, and Lyle was a good husband. I listened with the deaf ears of a selfish teenage girl, waiting, instead, for him to beg me to leave Lyle. I'm sure I would have, but he never asked.

At some point, I realized that Jimmy had many other women in his life. Coworkers and mutual friends later told me he had slept with somewhere between 200 and 300 women. It's a miracle I didn't contract an STD from him. I'm not kidding. But since other men had started paying attention to me, I was okay with his diminishing attention. In fact, the more I heard about Jimmy's other affairs, the more I pursued the thrill of the chase with other men.

I know now I have an addict's personality. Food had been my drug of choice my whole life. Once I stopped overindulging in that arena, I channeled my compulsive behavior into a new obsession—extramarital relations. I became a sex fiend.

The intercompany e-mail provided me with my next con-quest. Scott and I were colleagues who had begun flirting between typical office correspondences. When we were assigned to work on an account together, we often met for drinks after work to "brainstorm." One night he invited me back to his apartment. Without hesitating, I accepted his invitation. The first time we slept together it was pretty clear that our relationship was going to be pure sport-fucking. It wasn't about love, feeling important, or needing anything. It was fucking with no strings attached. I really, really liked it.

I wasn't interested in having an exclusive extracurricular fuck. Especially since Jimmy was sleeping with hundreds of other women. He had the nerve to tell me he wanted me to be exclusive to him. I found that rather amusing. Jealousy consumed him, which was absurd, given his track record. But he couldn't help himself and asked me constantly if I was sleeping with someone else. Since I liked sleeping with him, I'd lie and tell him he was the only one other than my husband, but he was never quite sure if I was telling the truth. He maintained a possessive double standard that was a little too macho for my taste. If the sex hadn't been so addicting, I would have cut things off then. But I had to have him, so I appealed to his huge ego by saying that he was the only man who was able to satisfy me.

Eventually, I just got fed up with Jimmy and walked away. He had served a worthy purpose—he'd given me confidence, taught me how to be assertive and take what I wanted from life. Which I did, repeatedly. But after I'd moved on, I still missed him. After all, he'd changed my life.

After Jimmy and Scott, Chris was my only other significant lover. He was an assistant in my office. In contrast to Jimmy, who had courted me with long lunches for a month before hitting on me, I pursued Chris with the sole intention of having my way with him. I was thirty-eight; he was twenty-five, a blond, blue-eyed baby who never knew what hit him. He didn't seem to care—what started as a one-night stand quickly evolved into a twice-a-week, seven-month affair. He thought I was single, and I preferred it that way.

When I was with Jimmy, I played the role of the cheating spouse. With Chris I assumed the part of sexual mentor. Everything Jimmy had carefully taught me I passed on to Chris, with my precise and enthusiastic touch. He told me that no one had ever given him head the way I did, and for the first time in my life, I believed it. I paid for our hotel rooms on the company expense account and wrote off everything: extravagant dinners, gifts, a night at the Ritz. I became his sugar mommy. Something about the power, control, and secrecy got me off. He wasn't very cultured, so it became quite easy to tease him with nice things. My motto then was simply, "Charge it!"

> *Something about the power, control, and secrecy got me off.*

Chris always worried that people would talk. He was right. Our colleagues figured it out even though we emphatically denied it. Seven months into our relationship, he started seeing someone else. It was inevitable. I was older, married, and never available on Saturday nights. But it turned out not to matter.

There were still three or four other guys from work that I could play with.

I found myself raising the stakes, embarking on a wild ride even more illicit than the one I'd been on. One time I did something really evil—I slept with a guy whose wife had just had a baby. I knew it was wrong, but he really wanted to get laid and I was happy to help. Then I took off my wedding ring and began the fine art of seducing my most valued clients. Sleeping with clients was taboo, but I felt invincible. When I pulled out of my driveway each morning, safely out of the reach of my husband and children, I put in a full day at the office and then led the life of a single, childless woman, ready for sex for a few hours each night. And then I'd return home.

I thrived on the drama, the kinky sex, and the escape. At home I was usually relaxed and happy, relieved of the day's tension by an orgasm or two. Sex became my after-work cocktail. Separating the two worlds was easy. Hottie salesgirl by day, sex kitten by dusk, but I was always a mother and a wife when I returned home at night. My home life was very relaxing compared to all the drama in the rest of my life. When I needed to break free, I would make a call or two, and then tell Lyle that I was going to dinner with a client that evening. I'd go to a hotel and fuck somebody senseless. Then I'd drive back home and sleep like a baby, curled up beside my husband.

The whole time I was having extramarital relations, I continued having sex with my husband at least two to three times a week so he wouldn't be suspicious of my activities. It was always, always routine. I didn't want my husband to ever ask, "Where did you learn that?"

Highly pleasurable addictions often start with a small transgression and then you find that you need more and more. Soon it becomes more than normal life can provide. I learned this at the company Christmas party one year, after downing a couple of double gin martinis. Two clients caught my eye and agreed to free me from the doldrums of the corporate world. They took me back to their hotel and fucked me every-which-way, simultaneously. I was too drunk to remember much, but I remember one moment of clarity, somewhere between all the sweat, hair, and legs, when I realized that two good fucks is far, far better than one. The next day I had to call on one of them as a business client, but I was so hung-over that I couldn't even face him. My assistant made my apologies. Clearly, my sense of self-restraint was gone.

Like all great things, there's a beginning and an end. I stopped working in sales, got lazy and, you guessed it, started gaining weight. Maybe subconsciously I knew that my actions were getting out of control and eating was the only way I could save me from myself. My husband has the morals of a Boy Scout and would not forgive me if he knew what I had done. Sometimes from my safe perch—sitting on a sunken chaise lounge, wearing the biggest sweat pants I can find, and munching from a bag of chips—I stare at him in awe and wonder what he did or thought during those countless evenings that I was gone. I can hear him telling the children, "Mommy's working late, again." He's always home at night, kissing the children on the cheek, and savoring every moment he spends with them.

My husband married an overweight girl, and never expected me to be thin. When I'm fat, home is the only comfortable place.

The other men, however, will not set eyes on me until I lose weight. It's ironic, but when I was thin, no amount of secret sex seemed to satisfy me. Now that I've gained eighty pounds, I will only sleep with my husband. I'm not working out at all these days, and my eating is pretty pathetic. The doctor diagnosed me with obsessive-compulsive disorder, which explains a lot of my self-destructive behavior. Sometimes I drink like a guppy and ponder the many slutty things I have done and concealed in the past. When this happens, I anesthetize myself with the food that serves as my current narcotic.

I harbor so many secrets. One of them is that I still fantasize about being the hottie who seduces her clients, or bending over a chair and having Jimmy fuck me in the ass. But lately, the only sex I'm having is with my husband, in the same bed at the same time in the same position, week after week. Welcome to married life.

7.

Beauty and the Beast

The Story of Theresa DeLuca

*T*heresa was a primary-school teacher from a small Mid-western town. She heard about my infidelity interviews from her girlfriend, who had heard about them from a friend of a friend. She asked me to meet her near her home at an Irish pub that was known for its wide variety of beers. Theresa said her first husband, Ian, loved the joint and since I wasn't going to get to meet him, I might better understand what kind of guy she had been married to by checking out his favorite hangout.

I spotted Theresa as soon as she walked in. A neat, practical-looking woman with brown hair in a short pageboy, she stood out from the other patrons—mostly men in jeans and flannel shirts who ordered their beers by the pint. Theresa was quite beautiful in a very natural, understated way—the only makeup she was wearing was a soft berry lip color. She stood about five foot six and was in her forties, but her slim figure made *her appear much younger. She wore neat trousers and a soft fleece jacket, completing her youthful look with a stylish leather backpack.*

Her air of optimism and good sense—from her clothing right down to her manner of speech—didn't jibe with my preconceived notion of an adulteress. She held out her hand, and, as if reading my mind, she said, "I know, I don't look like the other women you're talking to." I told her that every woman I'd met with had shattered at least one of my preconceived notions as to the kind of woman who is unfaithful.

We found a table away from the bar and ordered white wine and fried mozzarella sticks. Theresa even spoke like a schoolteacher, and as she told her story, I couldn't help noticing the contrast between her prim demeanor and her unconventional personal choices.

She said that her ideas of love and marriage had come from books and movies, as her parents were old-fashioned and had never discussed sex with her. They had set very strict limits for Theresa and her sister regarding boys, dating, and anything sexual. No miniskirts, no going braless, no going out alone with boys in cars. They were from a different generation and preferred silence to any kind of openness about what their developing daughters were going through. Because any acknowledgment of her sexuality was denied, the quest for sexual satisfaction became a major theme in her life. I couldn't help think that if women were as educated about the real facts of our sexuality as we are about reading and math, Theresa's path, for one, would have been a lot smoother.

∞

I HAD BEEN dreaming of having an affair for more than five years before it actually happened. My marriage was unbearably unsatisfying, and I repeatedly told my husband Ian, "This is it! I'm not your doormat. Clean up your act, stop smoking pot, or it's over." And he would, for a while. Things would be sweet for three to six months, nine at the most; then they would turn sour again. Ian would relapse, getting high every day and alternately becoming abusive or giving me the silent treatment. It was a vicious cycle that held me captive for almost twenty years. During that time I had two affairs—three, if you count what happened with my second husband.

I married Ian when I was twenty-five—old enough to know better. But I was pretty inexperienced. My parents had been so strict that I didn't date much. When Ian asked me to marry him, I was thrilled because I wanted a child. There was never any big physical attraction between us, but at the time I thought less emotion and more stability might be good for me. The marriage turned out to be a big mistake, but I got what I wanted most—a beautiful son, Jeffrey. Sure, there were some happy times, but Ian was not a very nice person. In fact, he was a shit. He was emotionally abusive, and back then I was easy to abuse.

He smoked a lot of marijuana and snorted cocaine from time to time. He was extremely moody—sometimes he wouldn't talk to me for days, but when he started talking, it was a constant litany of insults. I preferred the silent treatment because of the baby. It was important for me to keep peace in the house for his sake.

The sex was terrible. There was never any warmth or intimacy between us. This may sound crazy, but we were married for seventeen years, and he never kissed me; maybe a peck on the cheek when we were talking, but never any sexual kissing or foreplay. To make matters worse, he was a premature ejaculator. This was a tremendous issue for him—and for me.

In theory, Ian was interested in open relationships, but his sexual problems kept him from actively pursuing anyone. He didn't want to risk embarrassment or exposure, but he was very flirtatious with other women, right in front of me. The group we hung out with was very open sexually. Ian and I used to have Jacuzzi parties at the house, and we'd all go in the hot tub nude.

It's ironic that I got sucked into this type of scene, because I wasn't raised with any of this. My mother was a prude. I always thought of myself as one, too. But Ian's behavior must have had an impact on me: During the early part of my marriage, I surprised myself by fooling around with Seth, a friend of my husband's. We fooled around for years, but I never slept with him.

At our parties, Seth and I would wait in the Jacuzzi until everyone else paired up and left, and then we'd steal a few moments. Ian was always around, but I don't think he cared much, because he knew that we were just making out. He had an interesting attitude about it. If I'd gone out to meet Seth somewhere, privately, or if I had slept with him, Ian would have had a fit, but the fact that it was on his turf made him feel like he was a part of it. It was almost like he was giving his okay; it gave him a feeling of control.

Seth kissed me in ways that Ian never would—he was into it. I knew he wanted more from me, but he seemed okay with just passionate kissing, and it never went further than that. Our make-out sessions only happened at our parties. All evening long I would wait for the moment in anticipation, counting the minutes. I knew that Seth was waiting, too. He would come close to me and touch me or rub me.

Those brief moments with Seth caused intense anxiety for me—not because I felt guilty, but because I was waiting for more, desperately wanting more. This unreleased sexual tension went on between us for years, with no possible resolution. We could never have sex, because we were just playing among friends. So by the time I met Dusty, I was ripe for the plucking.

When our son, Jeffrey, was five years old, I decided to go back to school and get a degree in environmental science. I registered for my first college course, an ecological field study, and embarked on the real steps toward finding myself. I found myself, all right. I found myself longing more than ever for someone who truly appreciated me. I was desperate for an affair. That class taught me a lot—not only about water quality, but also about getting what I wanted.

I was thrilled when the instructor booked the class into a beautiful wilderness hotel for two nights, where we analyzed water samples and scribbled in our field journals. It was the first time I had been away from home in more than five years.

I didn't get out much because I had a child and Ian wasn't much fun to go anywhere with.

But my fellow students were a lot of fun. On our first night out, we went to a country-and-western nightclub. I had had plenty to drink, so I was way more outgoing and flirty than usual, and a local cowboy named Dusty started paying attention to me. He was cute, but more important, he was a great dancer. A typical sexy cowboy with his wingtip boots, tight Wrangler jeans, and Stetson hat—he knew all the country-and-western moves. I was intrigued by him. We danced, we drank, we flirted. My classmates were encouraging me, applauding whenever I whirled by in Dusty's arms. He suggested that I come home with him, and I said yes.

Dusty was appealing, not classically handsome, but cute in his own way. And he was interested in me. I remember driving down the highway in his truck with the windows open and the trees whizzing by. The Eagles song "Peaceful Easy Feeling" was on the radio, and he was singing out loud, to me. He was openly affectionate, taking my hand and pulling me close beside him. This ease of affection had a huge effect on me—probably way out of proportion to what he was actually doing. It made me aware of how barren my emotional and physical life was with Ian. It was springtime and I felt elated, as if I'd been cast in the most romantic movie. He made it very clear that he thought I was great, and it felt wonderful. It was the answer to all of my prayers—exactly what I'd been longing for, and what I needed to sustain me in my life.

The actual sex was a little bit disappointing. He was cocky about it. I take a long time to come and it takes a lot of effort to get me there. He was good about foreplay and passionate kissing but he set the pace for both of us, and when he wanted to move on, he just moved on—whether I was ready or not. I said something about it afterward, and he said, "Well, you're just going to have to learn to take care of yourself."

That is what they call a "red flag."

Still, he was definitely an improvement over Ian. He was clearly interested in me, even after the sex, so I was able to forgive the fact that he wasn't the most attentive lover. He wanted my number, so I gave it to him.

We stayed in touch. I went back to see him and spend the weekend with him whenever I could get away. I usually lied and said I was doing something for school and Ian never suspected a thing. Dusty would always take me out dancing, and it was great—in western-style dancing, there's a lot of partnering and touching, and he always seemed so glad to have me beside him. When I was dancing with him I felt beautiful and sexy, like Jennifer Lopez. I really blossomed under his affection. I didn't have a moment of guilt about Ian, but I did feel a little guilty about not feeling guilty.

The sex continued to be mediocre. Looking back, I don't think I was in it for the sex. I remember once reading about a beautiful countess who was being wooed by two men. The first man was incredibly handsome, intelligent, and rich. The second man was not as good-looking, smart, or wealthy, yet she chose him over the first guy. When asked why, she explained that when she was with the first man, she felt like she was with the most intelligent, handsome, and witty guy around. But when she was with the second man, she felt like *she* was the most beautiful, intelligent, and witty woman in the world.

That's how it was with Dusty. With him, I felt like the cute woman I'd always wanted to be. I was funnier, smarter, and more confident when I was with him. He wrapped his arm around me, held my hand, kissed my forehead, and I felt good. I'd always wanted to lose five pounds, and as soon as I met him, I did. I was finally happy in my own skin.

One time he surprised me and came to town just to see me. I lied to my husband and told him I was going to dinner and a movie with a girlfriend. I went to the hotel where Dusty was staying, and we were together until very late that night. The next day I lied to Ian again and rushed back for some afternoon delight. I didn't feel guilty at all. I felt I deserved it, because Ian had emotionally and physically abandoned me. This wasn't the way I had wanted my marriage to play out, but I was trying to make the best of things.

For the duration of our affair, Dusty and I talked a lot during the week. I could only reach him at odd times because of work and family responsibilities. I often called from a pay phone at school, just to feel alive. I was getting something so meaningful from our affair that even when I wasn't with him, it carried me through days and weeks at a time.

I was getting something so meaningful from our affair that even when I wasn't with him, it carried me through days and weeks at a time.

Our affair lasted almost one year. Then the whole AIDS thing started to break and I realized I didn't know much about him or who else he might be sleeping with. I told him I wanted him to get a test, and he was offended that I would even suggest such a thing. He declined, in the same manner that he declined when I would ask for more oral sex or longer penetration. Suddenly, there was a wall between us, which smacked too close to what I'd already had a lifetime of in my marriage. There was no give and take, no discussion, just: "You have to get over it." But I was different now. I didn't want to get over it. In fact, I refused to get over it.

Despite the way it ended, I'm happy that I met Dusty and allowed myself to get involved with him. We stayed in touch for a while, and he transitioned into a friend, but I didn't see him often enough to really miss him. My relationship with Dusty was one of the steppingstones toward finding my self-confidence. It was very validating for me. In my psyche, I had set it up so that I got what I needed, carried through with it, and stood up for myself in the end, so the benefits of our affair lasted long after we split up.

My second affair was years in the making. I met Blake back when I was only twenty-one, before I was married to Ian. From the first minute we met, we adored each other. He was a good, kind person and had been interested in me for years, but he was a petite man, which was a problem for me since I couldn't imagine being with a man who was shorter. I know now that this was ridiculous—that good things really do come in small packages.

Back then, I was young and stupid. Blake always told me he was five foot six, but I'm five-six, and standing next to me, he looked smaller. I didn't think I was ever going to get over my height phobia, so I closed myself off to the possibility of having

Blake as a boyfriend and developed a very strong friendship with him. We played volleyball and were part of a social group of friends who did things together—movies, barbecues, overnights.

One time we were all on vacation, sleeping in our clothes in a cabin after a long day of hiking. Blake and I were cuddled up in a corner together. We started to make out, which caught me by surprise, because I thought I had ruled out the idea of taking Blake as a lover. But that night I was surprised by how much more sensual he was than I'd ever imagined he could be. We curled up in blankets and explored each other, sweetly. He was a fantastic kisser. After that, we ended up dating for a while.

Back then, there were lots of things about Blake that bothered me. I thought he was a fuddy-duddy because he was always so cautious—covering up with sunscreen, and watching his intake of fats and calories. I had such silly ideas about life back then! Blake seemed more like a father figure than a man I should be dating. I was young and wanted spontaneity and adventure. By the time Ian came along, I was ready for a bad boy. At the time, I mistook his cold indifference for cool nonchalance, which made him mysterious and unattainable to me, so I chased him. This was a stage I could have done without, and one that lasted way too long.

But Blake and I stayed in touch, as friends. Shortly after I got married to Ian, he met and married Clara. We became a friendly foursome, getting together for dinners and movies. Blake and I sometimes danced around our mutual longing, but he was really trying to make his marriage to Clara work. They eventually moved to Hawaii.

Blake and I wrote often, and there were many intimate phone calls. We didn't always talk about our mutual attraction—sometimes we talked about movies or a funny thing Jeffrey did. Whenever we were on the phone I found myself thinking about what my life would have been like if he and I had gotten married. I imagined it being quite fulfilling. But it was just wishful thinking.

And then he and Clara moved back for a few years, and the four of us got together quite frequently. Ian and Blake became close friends, but I didn't like Clara; she was difficult, and she didn't seem to want to get along with me. She would also alienate herself from the rest of us. The four of us went on a vacation to Hawaii. While we were there we drove to see the waterfalls and packed a picnic, but Clara kept to herself.

During that trip, I had the attention of both Ian and Blake. The three of us shared so many wonderful memories. Clara was always off somewhere reading a magazine or talking on her cell phone to a girlfriend. I really enjoyed the time I was with Blake, even when Ian was there, too. On one occasion the four of us went to a big party and I came into the room after having a bit of wine. I was wearing a sexy sundress and feeling playful. For some reason, I sashayed up to Blake and looked right into his eyes. He returned my gaze and said something like, "You are my dream girl; you always have been."

I melted down into the couch, feeling drawn to Blake in a way I had never been before. Someone snapped our picture. I still have it, and I smile whenever I look at it. We were so happy that day. We were beaming. It seemed like we were enveloped in an aura, on the same wavelength and completely in sync. In that moment, it was enough. I didn't need to haul him into the next room to get hot and passionate. We had connected; we were soul mates and what we had was real.

From that night on, Blake and I formed a connection that was very deep. I finally acknowledged that I had the same strong feelings for him that he'd always had for me. It was time to explore our mutual feelings of lust and longing.

Blake and I went for lunch one day when I didn't have any afternoon plans; he suggested we go to a hotel. I didn't need to be persuaded. We drove to the first one we could find and then spent the remainder of that afternoon passionately making out. He wouldn't go all the way with me because of Clara. He took his marital vows seriously and felt it would compromise his integrity. I would have in a heartbeat, but he set the rules that day. It made me want him more than ever.

After that, it was a very long time before we had another chance for privacy. It was such a pity. Here was this wonderful man who I could easily have been with years ago! How much crap could I have avoided in my life if I'd only realized it back then? What would I be like now if I had been with a man who was nurturing and supportive instead selfish and destructive?

Then Blake and Clara moved back to Hawaii. My heart sank. He called me from there, and we continued our sweet conversations. We missed each other deeply. It was different than it had been with Dusty, because it wasn't just based on physical attraction and sexual need—Blake and I really loved each other. It was so bittersweet because Blake was so far away, and I had no idea if or when he'd move back.

It was as if Blake had just left me adrift, bobbing around on a sea of abuse in a very small boat. Blake and his wife worked together, so he couldn't call me from work. He would stop on the road to call me from pay phones. Sometimes we talked about how unhappy he was in his marriage. Clara was moody and unstable. She went on and off hormone therapy and was flipping out—having anxiety attacks and fits of rage, attacking Blake verbally, even physically. I wondered if she sensed that something was diverting Blake's attention away from her.

The phone calls abruptly ended. I didn't hear from Blake for a long time and I wondered why. I was afraid to call because I thought Clara knew about us and talking to me might make everything worse, especially for Blake.

I pined for him. He had been a good, true, loyal friend all those years and now I feared the worst: I'd lost our friendship. That was more painful to me than losing a lover; I had lost someone I had known since I was a young woman. It had been fifteen years. We had a history together—good times, bad times, funny times.

During that time, my marriage to Ian had become impossible. We had a boat harbored down in the marina, and I talked Ian into going down there to live on the boat, to give me some space. It was wonderful. I consulted a lawyer. She took my hand and said, "Come with me—I'm going to handle this thing for you. Everything's going to be okay." And it was. Finally, after seventeen years of ups and downs, Ian and I split for good.

A few months later, I met a man named Doug on a cruise that I took with one of my girlfriends. Doug noticed me right away and was instantly by my side, buying me drinks and telling funny stories; he was attentive and entertaining. Doug pursued me for quite a while before we became sexually involved. I was so confused by my separation from Ian, my feelings for Blake, and my desire to connect with a man I loved, I told him I needed to get to know him before we slept together. He was very understanding about my position. When we finally did make love, I was relieved to find that he was interested in pleasing me. He lasted a lot longer than Ian—which wasn't saying much—and was into kissing, but it still wasn't bells and whistles for me.

Doug was so different from Blake. He was a big man, at least thirty pounds overweight, so he had a big ol' belly, which was a turnoff. Whenever we had sex, his stomach prevented our hips from touching. It also made full penetration nearly impossible. Sometimes it felt as if there was a pillow lodged between us, and I couldn't get my skin to press against his where it needed to. I had a difficult time with that, but by then I was in my midforties and I told myself that sex didn't matter as much. I needed a man I could depend on. And he was just such a man.

Doug was enamored with me, and he was gaga over my packaging. That was fantastic for me. I was his prize, in a flattering way. Our relationship progressed, and we bought Ian out of the house, and made plans to remodel. Things were going well between us. Doug would have done anything I asked. It was good for my son to finally see what a functional, adult relationship was like. As much as I had tried to protect Jeffrey from my unhappiness, I always assumed he knew the truth about my feelings toward his father. If I have any regrets about my parenting skills, it's that I wasn't able to make my marriage to Ian more satisfying and therefore tolerable.

Doug was a good man, so I told myself I should get on with my life. But that didn't stop me from thinking about Blake, even though I hadn't heard from him. I decided that I wanted to marry Doug, even though we had only been together for one year, so I pushed the issue. We got married in Las Vegas so fast, we didn't have time to tell anyone, even Jeffrey. I wanted to break it to him slowly, to be sure he could handle it.

So there we were, with a big addition planned for the house, the plans drawn, the financing set, the marriage accomplished—and Blake called, out of the blue. He wanted me to come for a visit. Instead, I orchestrated a mother and son trip to Hawaii, telling Doug that it would be good for Jeffrey and me to take a vacation together—so Jeffrey wouldn't feel like Doug was displacing him. What I really wanted was to see what was happening, if anything, between Blake and me. I found out when we got there that he and Clara had divorced and he wanted to reconnect with me. I was out of my mind with happiness but I was worried about Doug. I also wanted to make sure that Jeffrey didn't know what was going on.

Jeffrey wanted to spend his days surfing, so Blake and I rented a room at a little hotel near the beach where Jeffrey was hanging out. The room had tropical rattan furniture and hibiscus prints everywhere. And there was a plumeria bush outside the window and the fragrance of that with the salt air made us feel like we were in paradise.

My dreams had finally come true. We had incredible sex—with bells, whistles, the whole nine yards. Blake was rock hard and stayed that way forever. It was everything I had always

107

imagined that the best sex could be. It was as if I was the star in the hottest love scene from a movie. It was all so perfect except now I was cheating on my second husband. Doug was a good man, but he wasn't Blake.

I left Doug for Blake, and we've been together ever since. We talk about everything. He's a happy man, and he continues to encourage me and boost my confidence. And he loves Jeffrey. He was the one who suggested that I go into teaching; he supported me through certification, and again through my master's degree.

Blake is now sixty-four and takes blood pressure medicine, which has changed the spontaneity of our sexual life. I'm the one raring to go, and he's the one who needs more time! But it's not the most important part of our relationship, anyway. When you achieve true intimacy with someone, everything is in balance. You don't need to concentrate on just one part to make up for the other parts you don't have. You can be truly satisfied and happy on all levels. We still enjoy a variety of things in life together. This was the man I was destined to be happy with. I'm just sorry it took so long to realize it.

8.

Ticket to Ride

The Story of Leigh Gardetta

eigh Gardetta and I ran into each other at Book Expo, where I was looking for a publisher for my young adult novels. Wandering from booth to booth was tedious and frustrating, and the bright lights made the convention center feel like an oven. It was nirvana to find a Starbucks coffee cart tucked in the corner. Who knew what a jewel of an interviewee would also be taking refuge there. I laid down my books on the counter to get my money out and ordered an iced Americano with a splash of low-fat steamed milk.

She appeared behind me in line, a thirty-something woman, ex-prom-queen-cum-surfer chick. She looked as tired as I felt. At some point her eyes landed on my books. Gesturing to them she asked, "Are those your books?" I nodded and stuck out my hand. She gave me a firm, confident handshake and, meeting my eyes, introduced herself. "Leigh Gardetta, paperback writer." "And Beatles fan?" I asked. We took our coffees over to a table and talked shop for a while—discussing the ups and downs of publishing.

With her sun-bleached ponytail and weathered skin, she looked as if she'd ridden a few waves since high school. I later learned that two kids from two different men, a string of bad relationships, and serial rejection letters from all of the major publishers had taken their toll on her. She hated the business side but writing always gave her hope. Her fantasy was to be the next J. K. Rowling.

As we chatted about our various projects, I told her about my infidelity research. Her interest was immediately piqued. "You'll want to hear my story," she said. "I don't believe in coincidences; we were meant to meet."

A few nights later we folded ourselves into an out-of-the-way booth at a trendy bistro with a bottle of Pinot Grigio. I ordered a spread of appetizers and asked the waiter to hold dinner until our interview was over. Then I leaned in and listened as Leigh told me the story of how she sought revenge on her philandering husband by cheating like a man.

∞

I HAD TWO one-night stands while I was married. Back to back. I know it sounds odd, but I was trying to make my marriage right. I thought that avenging my husband's indiscretions would make me feel better. . . . What a fool I was!

> *I thought that avenging my husband's indiscretions*
> *would make me feel better.*

It started with a trip to Palm Springs for a bachelorette party. It was a weekend of old friends and fun. Friday night we ate dinner at a hip restaurant. We were drinking, carrying on, reliving old memories, and having a great time. Around eleven we moved down the street to a nightclub with live music. I was just there to let my hair down—to dance and have a good time with my girlfriends. I'll dance with anyone, but I never cross the line, never let a guy touch me, and I've certainly never gone home with anyone. I fully planned on dancing the night away and crashing in my room, alone.

I guess plans are made to be broken. Shortly after we arrived, an attractive, muscular man named Bill . . . or was it Bob? . . . invited me to dance. He said he was a professional baseball player. The band was on break and the DJ was playing "Brick House." He led me out to the dance floor and started bumping and grinding in my direction. I went right back at him, pumped up by the music's beat. A couple of songs later we were both ready for a beer. I would have been happy to sit at the bar and nurse my drink, but he wanted to get right back on the dance floor.

The music got raunchier, and we started dirty dancing. He pulled me close to him, and I could feel his breath on my neck. Any figure flaws I was hoping my outfit would conceal were obvious to him. He was reading me like a book, in Braille. My friend Angie watched the entire spectacle from our table, Scotch in hand. As my partner spun me around, Angie looked at me, raising her eyebrows and her wedding ring. She thought I was a cock-tease and that I would never cheat on Robbie. I wasn't so sure anymore.

Robbie and I had met eight years earlier when I was waiting tables at Denny's. I was nineteen and single; he was thirty-six and married. He owned a men's clothing store across the street from the restaurant, so he would come in every day. Thanks to him and a few other big tippers, I worked my way through college.

Regular customers . . . you know how they talk . . . about the wife, the kids, the secretary. Nothing is off-limits. Right away he told me he was unhappily married. He was such a nice guy, I assumed it was her fault. Robbie and I really hit it off, but we were just friends. I never considered getting romantically involved with him; he was just someone to talk with when I was at work.

At the time I was seeing a guy who was definitely not marriage material. Sex was the glue that held that relationship

112

together, and thinking back on it, it was only enjoyable when alcohol helped me forget my long-term goals. One mistake led to another, and soon I found myself pregnant and alone. After weeks of indecision, I decided to keep the baby. Marrying the father was not a possibility; even if I had wanted to, he'd made it clear that that wasn't in the cards.

It wasn't easy to get up and go to work every day, but finances were a big issue, so I kept waiting tables until my doctor told me I had to stop. Saying goodbye to coworkers and customers, including regulars like Robbie, closed that chapter of my life.

After Molly was born, I did the single mother thing for a while—juggling a day job, child rearing and, every once in a while, a writing assignment. One day, when Molly was four, I took her out in the stroller for a walk, venturing toward the Denny's where I had worked.

Rounding the corner, I practically bumped into Robbie. He threw his arms around me, apparently as happy to see me as I was to see him. Molly had fallen asleep, so we sat on the curb and caught up for hours. He was divorced and much happier, he said, and felt like he'd been given a "Get Out of Jail Free" card. His life was finally where he wanted it to be, which probably explained his breezy, open manner.

Later that afternoon there was a message on my machine from him, asking if I wanted to have lunch or dinner sometime. I picked up the phone, cutting off his message, and pressed *69, a numerical foreshadowing of things to come. He came over that night for dinner and never left.

In the beginning we spent long hours in bed making love, reading the paper, talking. I was twenty-four or twenty-five and had lost interest in dating immature men my own age. Robbie was older, and he seemed to understand what it meant to be a parent. He had two children of his own, Abby and Travis, aged ten and thirteen. When we started going out, the kids were always around. We all dated together, going to the movies, playing miniature golf, visiting the tennis club, or just hanging out. When we got married, we had only one day alone on our honeymoon before we went back to our new, blended family.

I was happily married. I trusted him. We talked all the time. He always let me know where he was and what he was doing. Then the suspicious calls started. More than a dozen times, I picked up the phone only for it to go dead after I said hello. Robbie had been giving me some lame excuses and I even caught him in an outright lie or two. Then one day I couldn't find him and I sensed there was something going on. He left me no choice but to play private eye. I decided to lay a trap for him by coming home early from a trip with my daughter. He fell right into it.

I was five months pregnant with our son Thomas at the time, and I wanted to go up to the mountains and relax for the last time before the baby was born. My plan was to go for three weeks, with Robbie joining me for the second week. Even though Robbie said he hated the idea of being left alone and begged me not to go, I think he knew what was going to happen: he would spend the time I was away with "her." Not that I knew who "she" was.

So Molly and I headed north, and everything was fine at first. Robbie came up the second week as planned and we all had a good time together. But after he left, he started acting strange on the phone and I could feel in my gut that something was wrong; the writing was on the wall. It had been for a while, but I'd chosen to ignore it. He didn't expect me for another few days, so I drove home the next morning like a madwoman. A lack of hard evidence didn't assuage my fears—when you know, you know.

Inside the house, I started my search for the truth. A wine cork on the kitchen counter was the first clue. Beads of sweat stood out on my forehead and I started to hyperventilate. I put Molly in front of the TV with a Barney video, which kept her entertained while I did my best imitation of a possessed *War of the Roses* psycho, tearing my house apart looking for more clues.

There were two clean wineglasses in the dishwasher, and I flipped. Robbie never, ever drank alone. Neither did I. We were social drinkers, period. I looked around the bedroom without finding anything unusual, so I assumed he hadn't had sex in our bed. But I wasn't done looking. I wandered into the kids' room, where there's a double bed. And right there on the floor, just peeking out from the bed skirt, was a gold hoop earring. It wasn't mine, and it certainly wasn't Molly's.

As if that weren't damning enough, there was a condom floating in the toilet in the kids' bathroom. I couldn't breathe. I was twenty-seven years old, and pregnant. The idea that he could cheat on me, on our family, was horrifying to me. I had been totally and completely loyal. I wanted our baby. I thought he wanted it, too. He admitted much later that he didn't even want the baby. He was just going along with it to keep me happy. The sad thing about our marriage was that in his own, sick way, I think he loved me and wanted to keep our family together.

That night I confronted him about the wine, the earring, the condom. He finally confessed, saying it was a woman whom he had known from his single days and that it was a one-time thing. That was just one of a zillion lies he would tell me over the next few years. But I had an inkling of who the woman was. I was so out of my mind that night that I got her number from 411, picked up the phone right then, and called her. "This is Leigh Gardetta," I said. "You just fucked my husband." And then I hung up before she could deny it.

Robbie tried to stop me from leaving but I was outta there. I got into my car, drove to the beach, and took a walk down by the water to organize my thoughts and form a plan. Several hours later, having found no way out, I walked back to my car. I was trapped. I'd done the single mom thing, and it was hard enough with one kid. In a few months, I would have another mouth to feed. There were no other options. I went back. Robbie said he felt absolutely terrible about what had happened. "It was a mistake, and it will never happen again. I'm so sorry." I'd heard his lies so many times before, I was immune to them. Still, what choice did I have?

It took me five more years to leave.

At the bachelorette party, the night was growing old and my dance partner was showing no signs of slowing down. I was sharing a hotel room with Sharon, who was getting quite cozy with a ballplayer of her own. They were part of a group of base-ball players bragging that they'd come to Palm Springs for a weekend of fast women and fine dining. Weren't Sharon and I the lucky ones? Our ballplayers invited us back to their room for a final cocktail. I knew I was flirting with disaster, but I tagged along anyway. I formed a plan: I would use my hot ballplayer to get even with my husband. It was time to tie the score, wipe away his transgressions, and start with a clean slate. I thought some hot sex would help me overcome my anger so Robbie and I could move forward.

Okay, I'm an idiot. Of course it didn't play out that way. Bill and I had a drink in the living room while Sharon and her guy went at it in an adjoining bedroom. I felt like a voyeur—their grunting and groaning could be heard down the block. As soon as we'd finished our drinks, my guy took my hand and walked me into his room. He slid his pants down and pulled off his shirt. Then he ripped off my clothes, murmuring that he wanted to make love to me.

What happened after that had no relation to lovemaking. It was fucking. Plain and simple. It was rough and it was hard. There was no way I was going to have an orgasm, so finally I just faked one. Once he came, he rolled off me, reached for the TV clicker, and started channel surfing. He didn't even try to make conversation. I slunk out of bed and got dressed, feeling terribly empty. Is this what Robbie had felt? If he had, he never would have done it twice. Sharon and I walked back to our hotel room; it was around five in the morning. I took a long hot shower and then crawled into bed. I woke at noon, with a pretty bad hangover.

I longed to stay back in the hotel the following night and order room service and Pay Per View, but there was no way the girls were going to stand for that. We headed back to the main drag. . . . Girls just wanna have fun! Two drinks later,

I found myself flirting with an insurance salesman from Phoenix—Paul. He was in town for a convention but had the night off. Foreplay was better this time—at least he paid for my drinks and spent several hours engaging me in a few games of backgammon. He was pretty cute, with shaggy brown hair and the darkest blue eyes.

When they announced last call, he invited me to his room. I surprised myself by saying yes. It occurred to me that maybe the way I'd done it the night before wasn't the right way at all. Maybe the key was to feel comfortable with the guy you were sleeping with. Paul and I had talked about everything—his work, my marital problems, who we thought would win the upcoming election—and I imagined that sex with him could be fun. Maybe even fulfilling. I was still hoping it would provide a glimpse of why Robbie had strayed.

Turns out it didn't make a bit of a difference for me. Once the lights were out and we were horizontal, the guilt set in. I started obsessing about where this guy's dick had been and wondering if my party favor from this wonderful weekend would require medication. But my issues didn't have anything to do with him. Paul was a nice guy. As a matter of fact, I wound up telling him why I'd agreed to sleep with him. Still, my anxiety didn't subside, even after I'd returned home. If anything, it got worse.

I never told Robbie though, and he never found out. So much for revenge. When I got back I insisted we try marriage counseling, but he continued to lie to me, even in front of the therapist. Every once in a while, when Robbie was out of town,

I'd call and check up on him late at night. He rarely answered his phone. Deep down I knew he was still fucking around. I tried to make it work and be happy for the sake of our kids. But I was miserable.

Casual extramarital sex wasn't fulfilling for me, so how could it be for Robbie? He was playing with fire—surely there must have been a significant emotional component to justify putting his marriage at risk. I concluded that he didn't really love me because if he did, he wouldn't have needed to be involved with other women. The sacred bond that Robbie and I had shared was irreparably broken.

I left Robbie, but I didn't get into another relationship. Separating wasn't about being able to date someone else. I needed to get away from him so I could heal and try to find some sort of happiness. Robbie never understood. He thought I was looking for some young guy to screw when, in fact, I was completely celibate for a year.

Robbie immediately found someone else to get into bed with and spent a weekend with her. I know, because the hotel charge showed up on my Visa bill. I asked him about it. For once he told the truth. And then he asked, "Aren't you doing the same thing?" "No, I'm not," I said, but I don't think he believed me. I suppose if I still cared I would have done something to prove it to him. All I wanted at that point was to be free.

Red-Handed

9.

Sex and Consequences

The Story of Liz Wilson

I was sitting in a coffee shop with a friend, when a good-looking young woman came in, carrying a stack of bakery boxes. Fresh cookies. I could smell the warm chocolate and my mouth began to water. An amateur baker myself, I went to the counter to see what she was bringing in—it was a delightful assortment of treats, fresh from her oven. I admired her work, and bought some samples. "Can you really make a living baking cookies?" I asked. She laughed and said, "Well, I'm also a writer." I asked her what she was working on and told her about my book. Her face clouded for a moment; then she said, "I have a story or two about that myself." Her accent was soft and lilting—pure Texas. She gave me her card, and we agreed to meet and talk.

The next week, I met Liz at a coffee shop in an exclusive neighborhood near the beach. She brought me a small box of goodies, tied with a string. I was immediately impressed with her. She had talent . . . and good looks. With her cascade of thick, strawberry-blond curls, a dusting of freckles all over her peachy skin, and a robust, curvy build that looked great in her tight jeans and fitted shirt, she was truly adorable. She wore oh-so-chic low-heeled boots, and she fit right in with the trendy crowd. Despite her urban look, I could easily picture her astride a horse in cowgirl boots and a hat.

The other thing that impressed me was her obvious youth—barely twenty-three, bright and fresh. She spoke freely, with a frank sense of humor about her own situation. Like a lot of Texans, she knew how to spin a tale.

MET MY husband, Marty, when I was eighteen years old. It was spring break of my freshman year in college. He went to school near where my family lived; he was the best friend of one of my old boyfriends—the only one who had ever broken my heart. I'd go home from school to my parents' house, and moon around endlessly over this lost boyfriend. He kept stringing me along, hanging out with me, and telling me how great I was. Then he dumped me and left me heartbroken. Sometime during the mooning process, he introduced me to his friend Marty.

I don't know if it's because I'm short, but I'm attracted to tall guys. Marty met my height requirements. He was perfect—

six foot one. He'd played basketball and was in good shape, if a little on the rangy side. Big old size-twelve feet, long arms, and fingers twice the length of my own.

On our first date, he told me that he loved me. I was like, "Oh wow! I love you too." I thought he meant he loved me as a person, the way we told each other in church every Sunday. I really just liked him.

He was a fundamentalist Christian, which kind of freaked me out. I come from a Methodist background. We can do everything. As long as you don't kill anyone, you're okay with God. But Marty said we couldn't have sex; he just wanted to pray together. It was odd, but you do hear weird stuff like that when you're from Nowhere, Texas.

I look back now and realize that the problem was that I loved him as a friend, not as a husband. I wasn't old enough to tell the difference. I was never significantly attracted to him. I liked him because he was nice, different in a quirky kinda way, fun to be around—and tall.

We dated through spring and then I came home for summer break. That summer with Marty was very eventful. He finally decided it was okay to have sex after all, so I lost my virginity, in the front seat of his truck. Then we moved into the bedroom, where my mother walked in on us having sex. All she could muster was, "You better be using condoms."

Meanwhile, I was also on the verge of a fling with my roommate back at school, who kept calling, kept writing me letters and funny postcards, and kept me linked to the college world I missed so much when I came back home. Naturally, I neglected to mention to Marty that I had feelings for my roommate.

And then, out of the blue, my father died, and my mother proceeded to have a nervous breakdown. Marty was right there for me, in the thick of things, with the funeral, my mother's medical needs, and both sides of the family coming and going. We were able to sneak off for "quiet time" in my bedroom, on my grandma's old-fashioned double bed with the shades pulled down, on top of Gran's heirloom quilt. Marty seemed to think it was a worse sin if we actually got under the covers. It was nevertheless an improvement from the truck. Sex with him was okay, but it wasn't phenomenal. I thought that's how it was supposed to be, just kind of okay. I didn't have any real experience, yet. He seemed to like it just fine. But I never felt quite comfortable, whether half-clothed on top of my childhood bed or lying across the front seat of Marty's pickup truck. My mom started to like him, once she got over her nervous breakdown. She still loves him; they talk all the time. He was the son she had always wanted.

That fall, I went back to school and fell in love with my roommate. I was living with him and one of my girlfriends. He was my first exciting relationship. It was like that show *Three's Company*—except Jack gets to sleep with Chrissy. I was Chrissy. My roommate was Jack.

I didn't have a sense of responsibility when I was at school. I didn't want to think like a grownup. I never balanced my checkbook, for instance—so Jack would do it for me. He even did my laundry. It was ridiculous! Still, I thought we had a great thing going. I just wanted to read and have exploratory sex with Jack after a hard day of studying. Sex with Jack was like a good book, with a lot of interesting chapters.

College was an ideal time in my life—but not very realistic compared to what I had left behind. At home, I had a painful past and, after the death of my father, an uncertain future. It never occurred to me that what I had at college could be real and that I didn't have to live the life my mom expected of me.

No one told me what to expect or what was coming next in my life. Before I knew it, one year went by, then two. I was almost a senior, and Jack and I were still having sex every day, living with our roommate, and answering to no one. Jack was my best-kept secret. Marty rarely came to mind, unless he called. I never even told Jack about Marty.

The summer after my junior year, I turned twenty-one. On my birthday, Marty and I went out to dinner to an Italian place. I was excited because I love good food. After dinner, we drove around, going nowhere. Marty would always do weird things like that, so I didn't think much of it.

We went to this stock tank—like a pond—and there was a gazebo nearby, with ducks everywhere. Not only were there ducks; there was duck poop—piles of it. I was standing there in a dress, watching him scoop mounds of duck poop off the bench in the gazebo. He insisted that I sit down, even though I said I'd rather stand. He laid his jacket on the bench, sat me down on it, knelt, and asked me to marry him.

It didn't occur to me to say, "I'm not ready for this." I just said, "Yes." Mostly, I think, out of shock.

All right then, I thought. I'll get married. Most of my high school friends were already married. I didn't realize that, like Nancy Reagan advised, I could just say no. My life at school seemed like a dream that had never really happened once I came back home. Choosing to leave a small town is never easy—there's pressure to stay from every which way. My town was so remote, so removed from anywhere else in the world. I often wondered why I didn't choose to stay on the other path?

All of a sudden, my life became a whirlwind of wedding plans—the dress, the bridesmaids, the flowers, the booze, what my mother was going to wear. . . . It was like a monster, or a disease that spread out of control. To me, it never seemed real. In Texas, you have a cake and punch wedding, and then you have the real wedding. We planned both weddings, and it was going to cost an absolute fortune. Marty just said yes to everything. I could tell him that the moon was purple and he would say yes. He helped with whatever detail I set him to. He was always so nice. Too nice.

After two months of more and more wedding frenzy, and less and less fun, it dawned on me that I was getting antsy about the whole wedding thing. Our sex life was already a disaster, which I attributed to too much stress and not enough privacy. Marty let me boss him around all day, then took me out to make out in his truck all night. I said, "Mom, I don't think I should be doing this."

My mother said, "Be sweet to him and he will always love you and take care of you."

That was little comfort coming from her, because she had barely tolerated my dad, who was the biggest cheater known to man. We would come home and there would be a glass of wine with somebody's lipstick on it and pink panties in the bedroom. Mom believed it was just part of being married. She wanted me to have a secure life, but security is not the right reason to get married when you're twenty-one.

My parents had hated each other. Dad, back then, had been a raging alcoholic and Mom had been the enabler. My brother was the victim child, and I was the hero. My dad would reward me with $10 a week every time my name was in the local paper. Sometimes I would rake in more than $100, because I did every extracurricular activity imaginable, just to get out of the house. That's why I started reading—it was the ultimate escape from my dysfunctional family. I loved the freedom I'd had while in college. But what was I doing with it? Wasting it away.

My mother spent $40,000 on our wedding. In my town, that's a lot of money. It was enormous. I had nine swigs of Jack Daniels before I met my bridesmaids at the salon. I was drinking right out of the bottle, hoping to drown my nagging sense of foreboding. The stylist was spraying my hair with Aqua Net when suddenly I snapped out of my stupor and asked myself, "How can I get out of this?"

Walking down the aisle, I scanned the church for exit doors. But there was no escape—I was in too deep. After the ceremony, I threw the bouquet and hit someone in the face. As we left the church, Marty put his hand down, and his wedding band fell off his finger and rolled away. We all watched it roll under the limo. Half the wedding party dropped to their knees because the limo was parked over a gutter grate, and the ring was teetering on the lip of it. When somebody snatched up the ring and handed it to Marty, I knew I was doomed. We didn't even have sex on our wedding night. There were people coming in and out of our room until four in the morning. I finally fell asleep on the floor. The next morning, as we pulled away, Marty realized he didn't have the plane tickets. He called his best man, who had to break into the church to get them for us.

It was an icky honeymoon, at a big Caribbean resort full of men in Speedos who had no business wearing such skimpy suits—men with gold chains and too much chest hair. We went on one of those booze cruises where you go snorkeling, and Marty started drinking. He had no tolerance for booze. He was yakking off the side of the boat, tossing Amaretto Sours. What kind of man drinks Amaretto Sours?

I told him we should've just gone to the pool at our apartment; we didn't have to spend a couple thousand dollars to puke on the beach in another country. It was boring. He wasn't interested in doing anything. I think he felt a little overwhelmed because he hadn't done a lot of traveling.

When we came back, my last year of school was about to start, so he moved with me into our own place. I left my sitcom world with Jack in much the same way any TV bimbo would have: with little to say and barely an intelligent thought in my head.

Marty and I already didn't get along, but marriage was something I was trained to subject myself to; like a textbook, I felt it was meaningful, somehow. But I would get frustrated with him for nothing. He'd say, "I'm sorry, I didn't know I did that. Let me make it up to you. I'm going to buy flowers." It was sweet, but he didn't stand up to me. He was so accommodating; it drove me mad.

Sex with Marty went from bad to worse. I called him my three-minute miracle, because if he made it to three minutes, it was a miracle. Forget his trying to find my clitoris—it was like someone searching for a marble under three blankets with a giant hand. That's what happens when you marry a virgin—they don't know what they are doing. No amount of literature, pornography, or lubricant could help us. I even went to a gynecologist, thinking maybe there was something I was doing that made things worse. She said I was fine.

> *No amount of literature,*
> *pornography, or lubricant could help us.*

We had other problems, too. I was a triple major: English, psychology, and business law. I would write a short story for one of my classes, and he would freak out, as if whatever I wrote—which never included him—really happened. Marty and I had nothing in common; he did not stimulate me in any way. After months of not getting along, I told him we had to go into counseling. He wouldn't go—he said he didn't think there was anything wrong with us. When I graduated, we moved back to our hometown. Marty got a job, and my mother was helping to support us; but he didn't want me working. He preferred that I just sit around the house and be the missus. When I had finally had enough, I got a job at the sports bar owned by Marty's father, and started making friends. Marty insisted that I get a pager and then he called me all the time. It was like having a tracking device.

Then I met somebody at work. Evan was promiscuous; he would sleep with anything. He was known as Evil Evan. Not only was he evil, he was a compulsive masturbator—and the antithesis of Marty. I was attracted to him instantly.

Chemically, we had sparks. He was always willing, and I

was his boss. I would tell him to do any nasty chore around the bar, and he would do it.

Evan would come for dinner, and hang out with us. Marty didn't feel threatened by him, because he knew him. But I started getting in trouble at work for talking to Evan too much. It doesn't look good for the boss's daughter-in-law to be hanging out with the wild and crazy bartender.

One evening, when Marty was out of town, Evan showed up at the door and said, "I didn't want you to be all alone." We watched *When Harry Met Sally* and drank vodka. Evan and I wound up having sex on my living-room floor. It was really good.

I was transported back to my days of carpet sex while doing homework with Jack—only this was even better. Evan not only did everything I told him to, but he told me to do things to him—and I loved it. He knew where everything was and how to use it. It was such a relief. I closed my eyes as tight as I could, and reveled in the simplicity and pleasure of casual, skillful sex.

But afterward, once I stopped panting, I got upset about it and threw up. Evan held my hair back while I was puking, and said we didn't have to tell anyone. That helped the fear, but it didn't help the guilt.

The guilt faded when deeper physical needs resurfaced. I slept with Evan a couple more times, once I was over the initial shock of cheating on my brand-new husband. At the same time, I told Marty we had two choices—either we go to counseling or we separate. He ignored me, so I struggled to get his attention. He had told me once that he would never marry a woman who had a tattoo, so I went out and got a tattoo.

I found myself seeking trouble wherever I could find it, out of resentment, boredom, frustration, or all three. One night, I ended up in a gay bar making out with a woman. She had one hand in my shirt and one hand in my pants, necking all over me. It was hot. I was determined to have fun with any warm body available, and there she was. Her name was Christy. She was a standup comedian and wore a perfume called Happy.

I came home late that night with Happy all over me, and a second tattoo, but Marty wasn't there.

There was a note on the door that said "I know everything!"

He and my mother had rooted through my notebooks and private journals, where I wrote everything about my married life. My journal revealed how conflicted and upset I was, how attracted I was to Evan, how my husband wasn't paying enough attention to me, and what a terrible lover he was.

It was ugly.

The moral of that story is, never write down anything that could incriminate you. Or if you do, shred it or set it on fire, but do not save it.

So, there I was at twenty-two, with a husband gone off after finding out I had cheated on him. I went into counseling and found myself complaining to a complete stranger about Marty's rutting and grunting like a pig, and the ingrown hairs on his ass, among other things, but it didn't seem to help much.

My mother started leaving nasty detailed messages about what she thought of my character. She left more nasty detailed messages with my shrink. I was not even twenty-three, and I'd been married and divorced. All my friends were married and having babies, and my mother had teamed up with my ex-husband to violate my privacy and destroy whatever was left of my marriage. I declared a temporary moratorium on Evan.

Marty came over one day, crying. It was so sad. I held him. He told me he was living with his parents. I am mud to them now. I will forever be the sinning, cheating daughter-in-law. There is no going back; family never forgets. His parents even sent my mom a bill for the divorce.

I told Marty he should find somebody else, and it wasn't long until he came to tell me that he had. Or, she found him. She was a hometown chubbette from his church, with really bad acne. Down and out as he was, he didn't stand a chance when she swooped in to save him.

Inevitably, Evan and I started dating again. He was very creative—a photographer, a writer, an artist. Artists are weird. They hang their dirty laundry out to dry and then sell it as art. Evan wrote a poem about the first time he saw me. Like anyone would really care. That sappy poem really got to me, though. No one had ever written anything about me before. We slept together the night he read it to me. He told me he loved me while we were having sex. He seemed so sincere, I believed him. That was my mistake. I didn't really know him. It took a few miles of bad road and a lot of vodka before I did.

One day he announced out of the blue that he had Tourette Syndrome. Not so much the vocal stuff, but crazy mood swings, facial tics, and obsessive-compulsive behavior. He had to touch the doorknob five times, organize his DVDs five times, and touch the computer screen five times. He was big on fives. He would do bizarre things, and then blame his disorder. I also noticed that his friends were all girls. He didn't have any guy friends. He had majored in photography, and had done lots of kinky sex photo projects with random girls. I was haunted by something my mother had always said—"People who cheat with you will eventually cheat on you."

After a while, we decided to get married and move to LA, so we loaded up the U-Haul and got a little place not far from the beach. I found work as an extra, and doubled for a dancer in a major production. I made $4,000 my first week. It was great. Evan got a job working for the woman who had hired me. She only hired male assistants. It was all very incestuous.

We were happy when we first moved to LA, but we started having terrible fights, and the sex tapered off. One day I came home early to find Evan in front of my computer screen, watching a Britney Spears video and masturbating.

Later, I discovered that fourteen gigs of my twenty-gig hard drive were being used for downloaded porn, so I deleted it all. It was my computer, after all. I saw things that day that I have never seen before and hope to never see again. I even saw a woman with a horse dick in her hands. I couldn't believe my eyes. When he noticed that his icons were gone, he had an out-of-control, raging fit.

He started reading my e-mails every day and tapping the phone. We never had sex. I would go to bed alone and he would masturbate to Britney Spears.

I thought about killing myself, but I didn't have a sharp enough knife in the house.

Then Evan and two actresses hooked up at some party, did Ecstasy, and had a threesome; I didn't know this right away. I woke up the next morning because he was choking me in his sleep. He had his hands around my throat, trying to kill me.

I woke him up; we had a little talk about what had happened; and then we had sex.

Later that day, I was at Kentucky Fried Chicken eating lunch when he called to tell me that he had been cheating on me for a long time. I had never felt so far away from Texas in my life. I was miserable. Marty got married a week after his chubby, pimply girlfriend had his baby. Marty's wife would never cheat on him, and he knows it. I don't miss him often, but I do miss him when I am having a "poor me" day. There are a lot of days like that in LA. It is a very lonely place. Most of all, I miss having someone worship every breath I take.

To have a successful relationship, you first have to respect yourself and be mindful of who you are. When I was twenty-two and first cheating, I didn't have a clue about what I wanted or needed. Now I know it's okay to have needs and to talk about them, and it's okay for the other person to have needs. You do have to talk.

I'm in love again. He's twelve years older. Older works for me these days. We met at a cooking store and bonded over a hand-mixer. I was torn between two different models and he said, "In this case, faster is better." He's a gourmet cook. I've learned that a man who knows his way around the kitchen is usually damn good in the bedroom, too. We've been together for sixteen months, but he cannot say "I love you." We talk first thing in the morning, he calls me at least once during the day, and we even talk at night; but we only see each other three times a week—because he's married. Guess my mom was right when she said, "What goes around comes around."

10.

The Naughty Neverland

The Story of Reina Rogers

*S*ome women appear to have it all—intelligence, good looks, a sparkling personality. Reina Rogers was one of those women. Her life should have been perfect. And it was, until she made some bad choices. Now she's suffering the consequences and hoping that telling her story will save other women from making some of the same mistakes.

It was dark and rainy the night of our interview. Mutual friends had arranged for us to meet at a hotel near her home. I arrived before she did and staked out a table by the fire in the lounge. Shaking the evening's chill wasn't going to be easy. By the time I finally warmed up, Reina was well into her tale of two marriages and subsequent affairs. An elegant brunette in a satin skirt adorned with flowers and tulle, she would dab at her eyes now and then with a tissue. Three hours later I said good night to this smart, sassy sexpot—who had tossed aside her chance for *happiness as if it were last night's leftovers—and thought about how her hard-won insights could be valuable to other women.*

OR ME, sex was always a serious matter. Unlike a lot of people I've known, I was never able to take it lightly. Even though I grew up in the sixties, in the era of the pill, sex was always a big deal. I didn't date much when I was younger. When I met my first husband, David, I hadn't had many sexual partners, which might have contributed to some of our problems.

We met after medical school, during our residency training. He was safe, sober, reasonable, kind, and very smart. He usually kept his passionate side well hidden, but for some reason, I brought it out in him. All the nurses were after him, but he wasn't interested. He was wholly devoted to his work—a thoughtful doctor, and a wonderful man. I knew he would be a grounding influence, someone whose advice I could depend on in my own career. I was happy and proud when he proposed to me.

As far as sex goes—what did I know? I didn't have much experience. I really wanted to have a husband, a mate. I now see that our sexual appetites were completely mismatched. I'm much more of a sensualist; I like fine fabrics, interesting textures, good food, good wine—the physical pleasures of life. David was more . . . well . . . cerebral and clinical. He loved the world of ideas. He wasn't sexual or sensual at all. For him, sexual needs were something to be taken care of, not something to be savored. The missionary position was just fine for him. Well, it was fine with me, too, for a long time—when we were both busy, working, training, and advancing in our careers. He was good-humored and reliable, and we had a comfortable relationship.

The week before David and I got married, I was at a medical meeting out of town. A pharmaceutical company sponsored the conference, and they knew how to do it right. All the attendees spent a fabulous week at a luxurious five-star resort. Just what the doctor ordered—rest and relaxation and some light work to take my mind off the frenetic preparations that were continuing back home in my absence.

A couple of glasses of wine at the welcome reception left me feeling decidedly lighthearted and at ease when we all went in and found our seats for dinner. I had to stifle a groan of boredom when I heard the title of the keynote speaker's speech: "How to Run a Successful Medical Practice." As it turned out, the speaker was easy on the eyes, as they say, and his talk was actually quite inspiring.

The crowd had thinned out by the time I got the chance to introduce myself. Bobby and I bantered for a few minutes and then he asked if I wanted to continue our conversation in the hotel lounge—he was ready for a nightcap. Tickled to be having what I assumed would be my last drink with another man, and a very attractive one at that, I decided to splurge and ordered a Long Island iced tea. It was time to party! When some of our colleagues turned up at the bar, what had started as a tête-à-tête soon morphed into a lively after-hours celebration. Before long, it was past midnight. Having enjoyed the drinks and the flirtation, I excused myself, explaining that I had to get up early.

A few minutes after I was settled into my room, the doorbell rang. It was room service, delivering a chilled bottle of Domaine Chandon Blanc de Noirs champagne. A handwritten card read, "Call me if you want company. Bobby, 720."

I was totally in love with my David, and I had been unerringly monogamous for the five years we'd been together. Yet, with the wedding just one week off, the prospect of "forsaking all others" was starting to scare me. Maybe I thought I needed a last fling before taking the plunge. Whatever it was, I picked up the phone and invited Bobby to join me.

With the wedding just one week off, the prospect of "forsaking all others" was starting to scare me.

He knocked, and came in with a big grin on his face. I stood there like a deer in headlights. He took one look at me and asked, "You've never done this before, have you?"

He took my hand—the one with the diamond on it—and said, "You're worried about your engagement, aren't you? Well, then, we'll just toast the bride, okay?"

He poured the champagne and sat close beside me on the bed. I drained my glass and before I knew it, I was all over him! We fell back onto the bed, laughing. I was like a woman possessed; I had never been like this with David, in all our years of staid premarital intercourse. But something was different with Bobby. I had to have this man.

He very willingly gave me everything I wanted, and more.

It was the most rousing sexual experience I'd ever had. I had never been on top during sex before, and I loved it—as well as everything else we tried.

That turned out to be the first of a week's worth of evening sexual extravaganzas. I had a modicum of guilt, but it was outweighed by all that great sex.

When I said goodbye to Bobby at the end of the week, I thought I meant it. We had had a great time together, but I knew it absolutely had to be over. On the flight home, I started feeling horribly guilty. What if my fiancé discovered my indiscretion? What if he called off the wedding? My worries wound me up tight, and I spent a few long anguished hours in-flight questioning myself. It was such a relief when David met me at the baggage claim area with open arms. He seemed genuinely delighted to see me.

That Sunday, David and I got married. After a lovely wedding, we embarked on a tropical honeymoon. Browsing through the local shops, I found myself looking for souvenirs to bring home to Bobby. It wasn't a good thing to be thinking about another man while I was on my honeymoon . . . clearly there was trouble in paradise!

Marriage with David offered companionship and security, and the comfort of living with a parental figure. He was attractive to me in more of a "big picture" way, but our sex life was not great. I loved him—I still love him, but there was no passion in our relationship. It occurred to me shortly after our wedding that I might have married him for the wrong reasons.

In our society, there's no training for this kind of thing. How are you supposed to know how to pick a husband? What should a woman look for in a marriage? I didn't know, and I'm still not quite sure. My parents didn't give me any guidance; all they ever seemed to care about was my financial security, and that wasn't ever going to make me emotionally happy. So, if not financial security, then what should one strive for? Passion? Everybody agrees that passion is important at first, but it doesn't last; it can't be sustained for twenty-plus years.

A few months after the honeymoon, my medical partnership hired Bobby as a consultant. Talk about mixed emotions—I was so excited to see him again and so afraid that this was going to be very dangerous.

Bobby was in and out of my office every week, and of course, we picked up where we had left off. People say you can get someone out of your system by hopping into bed with them. For me, this just didn't work. Illicit sexual encounters with Bobby never dulled my interest—quite the contrary. It was a kind of conquest over my own inhibitions, and it gave me an incredible high. I found out more about myself during this experience than I had in all my years with David—like what it meant to have a G spot. My affair was like a bag of Lay's potato chips: "Betcha can't eat just one." From the first day of my marriage to the last, fantasies of Bobby consumed me. I would never be sexually interested in or satisfied by David. My love for him was more like that for a dear friend, especially in contrast to the relationship I had with Bobby. Sadly, my marriage to David lasted only a year and a half.

I didn't leave David because I wanted to be single; I left him because I wanted to be with Bobby. At the time, I felt an irrational urgency to settle down. After the split, I thought Bobby and I would bond immediately.

It took a very long time for us to become truly happy as a couple and to build a relationship of trust. We dated on and off for five years and at times even lived together. This period was painful for me, because Bobby was a committed bachelor and wanted to keep seeing other women. Believing that Bobby was my one and only true love, I never slept with anyone else during that time. My sex life with him was always enthralling, and I couldn't get enough. I was discovering more and more the roots of my own pleasure, and also making up for lost time. I think it was my passion and my total delight in our adventures that kept Bobby interested. We were well matched in our sexual needs and desires—we were passionate souls.

Bobby eventually asked me to marry him. I wasn't comfortable with his hesitancy, but I was desperate for it to work out, so I overlooked obvious signs that our problems were being swept under the rug. Certain aspects of my personality bothered him and he made no bones about it. I'm very dramatic; I get strident when I'm angry; I'm very verbal and tough on men who get close to me; I'm possessive and I'm jealous. Bobby didn't know how to deal with me when I was in one of my "moods," so he just withdrew. When he didn't feel like having sex, I took it as a rejection. Our passion wasn't what it had once been, but I had ended my first marriage because of Bobby and I'd spent five years waiting for him, so I was determined to marry him.

A few years into the marriage we tried to conceive. I really wanted to have a baby. With each passing month that I wasn't pregnant, things between us got more difficult. I bought a greeting card when I was about thirty-five that showed a harried, attractive woman at her desk with papers all over the place, holding her head in her hands, saying, "Oh my God! I forgot to have children!" At the time, it struck me as the funniest card I'd ever seen. That was exactly me—but it turns out it wasn't really funny. Infertility puts unbearable pressure on a marriage; it breeds overwhelming feelings of failure and a hatred for sex. After three years of struggling, we finally got pregnant. I felt blessed to finally have a child.

Two years later, in a therapy session, Bobby announced that he was no longer attracted to me. I knew that was a very serious admission, which we should have explored more thoroughly while we were in the care of a trained professional, but we dropped out of therapy because we were afraid to dissect it.

The extra ten pounds I was carrying didn't help, even though I knew that wasn't really the root of the problem. Bobby was no longer attracted to me because I was a very intense mom and my world revolved around our son. I nursed him for more than nine months, which was wonderful, but my husband couldn't handle it. He felt threatened, squeamish, and began to make comments like, "I can't touch your breasts anymore. They belong to the baby." My indifference to the day-to-day things of life, like paying bills and cleaning the house, also bothered Bobby. It would have been helpful to be good at those things, but I never quite figured out how to do it all. Bobby definitely harbored anger over what he perceived as my neglect of our home. Our sex life diminished rapidly.

I finally lost the weight and started to look much better, but Bobby still didn't show any interest in me sexually. After all we'd been through, that was the point in our relationship when we should have either broken up or grown closer together. But again, we avoided confrontation. It was too difficult to address our mounting marital issues—I think we were both afraid it would reveal that we shouldn't really be together. As it turned out, the marriage was destined to end with our worst fears realized.

Meanwhile, there was a man at work who did find me attractive. Kip was a brilliant surgeon and a stimulating conversationalist. Our attraction enabled me to avoid dealing with my marital problems. I began flirting with him as a much-needed distraction while I was pregnant. It was harmless at that point because I was about to give birth. But later, after my son was born, we were still flirting with each other. It felt like we were drawn to each other as if by magnetic force. I knew that we were destined to have sex sooner or later. I decided to take the plunge and sleep with him, thinking it would be a one-time thing and I could get him out of my system. I figured I would taste the forbidden fruit, realize it was no big deal, and that would be that.

Of course, it didn't happen that way. The first time we were together lasted for four hours. He was a magician in bed, and very bad—nasty and thrilling and completely uninhibited. He egged me on, encouraging me to do things and try things that I hadn't thought of with Bobby. He liked very tight, very sexy underwear, with lots of straps and laces; he liked it when I wore stiletto heels right into bed. I could be as naughty as I liked—I felt like the star of my own porn movie. Illicit sex with Kip was like heroin addiction; I couldn't live without him. I lied to my husband and anyone I needed to in order to be with Kip as often as I could. I craved the rekindling of my sexual side, which the chores and responsibilities of married life had extinguished.

*I craved the rekindling of my sexual side, which the chores
and responsibilities of married life had extinguished.*

By then I'd found another therapist. When I first told him that
I was contemplating having sex with a dazzling, brilliant, interesting man who I had met professionally, he said, "So, you're going
to take a sledge hammer to your marriage?" I was very offended
by that, but if anything, that was an understatement. Anyone who
deludes herself into thinking that cheating is okay is sadly mistaken. If you don't want to decimate your marriage, think long
and hard before you do what I did. Talk to your girlfriends, or
your mother, or simply tell your husband that you feel unloved,
invisible, unwanted, desperate—anything! Just don't do it.

At the time, I wasn't capable of absorbing what my therapist
was saying. So I continued on with Kip for many years. I was so
drawn to him that I couldn't stop, no matter what happened. He
was single, dating, and not using protection, but I didn't care
enough to protest. Everything was second to the rush of sneaking off with him and escaping into the naughty Neverland we
had created together. There was a sex shop across town where
we often met; he picked out things that he wanted me to try on,
and then we went to his place or a hotel for one of our fantasy
sessions. Part of the thrill for both of us was the knowledge that
none of our colleagues knew about our secret, kinky life. I was
addicted to him both physically and emotionally and became
completely uninterested in sex with my husband. Even though
Bobby was a lovely man, a good provider, and a fabulous dad, I
couldn't stand things the way they were any longer. I was trans-
fixed by Kip and felt I had to come clean with Bobby.

146

I said, "I'm having an affair and I'm telling you because it's rocking my life and we need to go into counseling and talk about this." He was shocked. He had absolutely no idea—that's how little attention he paid to me. He lost interest in the passionate side of me once we got married and that's too bad, because he really could have enjoyed it, as he had when we first met.

Ending our marriage seemed like the right thing to do, but Bobby wanted to stay married to me. He wasn't happy about the affair but he thought we should raise our son together. Despite our problems, he was a prince of a fellow throughout our marriage.

At the urging of the therapist, I didn't see Kip for about six to eight months. But then it grew increasingly impossible to stay away from him. I fell back into him like a drug addict into her fix. I was just too emotionally involved and accustomed to sneaking around to stop myself. I finally just threw in the towel and told my husband I couldn't go on. Bobby and I divorced very quickly, because by then he was fed up.

Kip and I tried to build a relationship for a couple of years but it was an absolute disaster. He had major psychological issues, which I had known about all along, but that didn't stop me from trying to keep us together. He could never get out of the fantasy; he couldn't perform without props. In fact, he was impotent without his toys and accessories. Later, he started experimenting with drugs that he thought would increase his potency, but he didn't seem interested in me unless I was all tricked out and trying to arouse him. Our relationship was always turbulent, to say the least. We broke up at least a dozen times before things finally came to an end. Our sexual life was stimulating and arousing, but our personal relationship left me feeling impoverished.

Surviving the wild ride of such ecstatic highs and unbearable lows was very hard on me. When I was finally able to let him go, a close friend said to me, "You have been a doormat to this guy for years. It's so unlike you, almost as if an alien has inhabited you for a very long time"—and she was right.

It's easy to see how things go by the wayside when you're sneaking around. There is a reason why extramarital sex is so much better than marital sex. Secret lovers never see your dirty laundry or bad moods; they only see you made-up, at ease, and free of life's daily burdens. I was always eager to escape into the realm of sexual absorption. It's easy to have incredibly hot sex when there is nothing else to juggle. Orgasms are self-rewarding. I didn't love Kip, but I was sexually addicted to him, and apparently very needy at the time. It seemed I'd found my soul mate. Sadly, I was mistaken.

It's been three years since Kip and I have seen each other. I still wish I knew what he had wanted. Throwing away my marriage with Bobby to be with Kip was a huge mistake because it now seems Kip was only interested in having a relationship with me while I was married to someone else. It was very hurtful to realize that he could walk away from me completely unscathed. For me, the whole thing was destructive. The ultimate punishment was his moving on. I guess I got what I deserved. Time has taught me that marriage is sacred and worth fighting for. I learned this lesson too late to help me save my own marriage.

It kills me to think about what a mess I've made of my life. I'm single, forty-eight, and I've been married twice and unfaithful twice. Both times I cheated on my husband with a single man who I got passionately involved with. Ruining two marriages is proof positive that all the choices I've made with regard to my husbands and my lovers have been bad, if not outrageously stupid. David and Bobby were wonderful husbands, each in his own way. I was the one who was bad. I have the classic bad-boy syndrome. Many women have affairs, live with themselves, and rationalize it, but for me, my behavior has become a source of great agony and shame.

It's possible that my proclivity for doomed relationships started because my mother was horrible to me. She disowned me when I was seventeen after finding out that I was sexually active. She actually gave me the choice of either staying with my boyfriend or having a mother. Raging hormones and great sex led me to choose the boyfriend. My mother lost forty pounds and had a nervous breakdown. Intellectually, I understand now that my mother had serious problems—it's not natural for a mother to reject and disown her daughter. It hurt deeply for many years, but then the hurt turned to anger.

I'm still trying to work out why I made such bad decisions. Why are some women able to control their impulses and let them play out in their minds instead of acting on them like I did? Self-discipline, control, acting like a grownup, realizing that you have fantasies but shouldn't engage in destructive behavior . . . these are all key functions of a healthy marriage. It all makes sense now. Women considering an affair should enjoy the fantasy, go crazy with it—even flirt—but not allow themselves to get into a situation where it's inevitable that they'll sleep with somebody. And no one should ever feel bad about having a fantasy, because we all do. Men *and* women.

I grew up believing that biologically men are incapable of being faithful—that they have to "sow their seed," and that women are programmed to nest. But I'm sorry, we women have all the same senses men have. Which is fine as long as you can practice impulse control. I probably acted on my sexual impulses as a way to express my unhappiness and loneliness.

We all have to be careful out there because life can be treacherous. The prospect of an affair is so incredibly appealing and seductive. The sex can be as intoxicating as the most dangerous narcotic, but you have your whole life to live. Hot sex will not get you through the weeks, months, and years of raising a child, building a career, a life, a family.

Something happened to women my age. We grew up thinking Mr. Right would come along, we'd get married, and live happily ever after. Then the career boom suddenly reared its head and we were expected to become working women for the first time in history. On the one hand, we had to find Mr. Right and be a happily married woman. On the other hand, we had to fulfill ourselves professionally and be incredible. Oh, and let's not forget the need to have children and nurture a family.

I work full-time now out of necessity. My mortgage is steep, so I go to work before dawn three days a week and work nine to five, two days a week. Part-time work would be much easier, but I don't have that luxury. I've made a vow to myself to never betray a man again. At this point I'm allergic to the idea of cheating. Thinking about my behavior makes me sick. Infidelity is not sexy. I urge women to seek therapy rather than trying to escape from their marital problems.

I often think about the fact that when I was about to leave

Bobby for Kip, my therapist tried to talk me out of it. I'm still haunted by his words. He was treating another patient who had left two husbands and ended up alone later in life. She would often tell him how much she missed her "boring husband." I can still hear my therapist telling me this story, because I feel the same way. Why couldn't I hear him when he offered me what I now recognize as much-needed advice?

I miss being married to my second, boring husband very much. With any luck, we can still work it out. Given another chance at marriage with Bobby, I would work hard to try to spice it up. I would look for a balance between the high highs of infidelity and the monotony of monogamy—to keep it interesting, fun, and exciting, however I could.

Bobby and I have been divorced for five years. Nobody can figure out why we aren't married anymore because we still get along so well. As long as it's a possibility to get back together with Bobby, I won't abandon the idea. I brought it up to him recently and he agreed to have a conversation about it.

We both have fears and concerns, but I'm willing to make serious changes. Most important, I would promise to love, honor, and obey Bobby, which would be good for us and good for our son. I can't say for sure that this will make me happy, but I desperately want to try. I've learned the hard way that one person can't fill all of my needs, and that's okay. I bought into the idea that I'd find the perfect mate who would fill my soul, satisfy my friendship needs, my emotional needs, my intellectual needs, my sexual needs, all of my needs—but I never found it. My female friendships have lasted longer than both of my marriages combined and I'll love these women until I die. How have I managed to sustain those relationships? By not expecting them to be everything to me. If only I could have applied the same standard to my husbands.

It is just my son and me now. It's not easy being a single parent. It's too quiet at the dinner table; we always end up turning on the TV. Bobby and I have as good a situation as any divorced couple I've ever encountered, but I live with great sorrow because I get to see my son only half the time. The only good news is that my ex and I co-parent amicably. Those first few years after we split up, I felt as if I were on a bed of fire. Sharing custody was terribly painful, but the guilt of knowing I was responsible for breaking a trust and tearing my family apart was overwhelming. It wouldn't have been fair for me to ask for more than 50 percent custody, because my son needs and deserves equal time with his father. In hindsight, the breaking up of my family was too high a price to pay for great sex.

I see my ex-husband every day because of my son. We go to the same dinner parties and have many of the same friends. Neither of us has remarried. I've always thought he was cute, and it seems as if he has a newfound attraction to me now that we're no longer married. I'm excited about the prospect of getting back together someday and not just dreaming about it. His hesitation stems from lack of trust.

Right now, my ex-husband and son are away in Europe. I'm planning to meet up with them next week. We'll be together with a bunch of other people, although we won't be sleeping together or even be in the same room. It would be wonderful if being away could help spark a romance between us. Maybe it's a bit too optimistic of me, but hope springs eternal.

11.

Round and Round She Goes

The Story of Keisha Jones

I first met Keisha Jones at a hair salon in a hotel where I was staying. She was applying color to a customer. I was having my hair done by another stylist, and talking about my search for women who'd been unfaithful. "If you know anyone," I said, "please give her my number."

My stylist turned her head in Keisha's direction. "You should talk to Keisha over here. She's got a helluva story." Keisha thought about it for a minute. "Why not," she said. "Do you have to use my real name?" Reassured it would all be confidential, she agreed to an interview. I said we could do it wherever she felt most comfortable. She chose the ice-skating rink near her house.

The next night we met at the rink's ticket booth. It was a hot summer night, but the cold breath of the ice chilled me to the bone as we laced up our skates. I had hoped to sit and *talk for a few minutes, but before I knew it, Keisha was out on the ice flying around the rink, looking adorable in her short skating skirt. She had great legs and a gorgeous backside, and everyone watched as she warmed up, skating backward, forward, and then letting fly with a few spins and axels in the center of the rink.*

A petite woman with a cheerful smile, Keisha wore her hair in cornrows that hung down to her shoulders. Men flocked to her, trying to keep up as she moved around the rink, as if every inch of it were hers. Occasionally, she slowed down to accept an outstretched hand from one of her admirers and do a couple of laps of pair skating. It was wonderful to watch.

Unsure of myself after years away from skates, I hugged the rail until Keisha came to my rescue. She pulled me toward the middle of the rink, excited to share her passion for skating. Her steadiness on her feet and her secure grasp of my hand helped me to find my balance. Before long, I was right there with her, all on my own, working up a sweat and feeling exhilarated by the exercise.

When the Zamboni came out to repair the ice, we retired to the snack bar for a cup of hot chocolate with marshmallows. We settled down in a corner and I pulled out my tape recorder. I had a feeling Keisha's story was going to be a page-turner, and I wasn't disappointed.

∞

NEVER HAD the chance to get to know men before I got married because I was trying not to fornicate. I was doing the religious thing. When I was younger I was never allowed to go out with guys. My father was a Baptist minister, so we were very religious and my mama didn't let me have boyfriends. I was supposed to save myself for marriage. That was that. Now I'm making up for lost time.

It's easy to pick guys up. Most of the guys I know now, I know from the skate rink. A few years back, when I was with my first husband, I kept my skate life and my sex life separate. If I wanted a guy, I looked in other places. That changed over time.

My first husband, Ron, was a very religious white man. I met him at a vacation Bible camp one summer. We were both counselors. Neither one of us believed in premarital sex, but we ended up doing it, right there in the counselors' cabin. Afterward, he wanted to pray; I wanted to enjoy the moment.

He said, "We shouldn't do this any more," but I was just beginning to realize what I'd been missing. Every time we were alone—and I made sure we were a lot—I would touch him, all over, everywhere. I am sure nobody had ever touched his dick before. That would get him so hot that he couldn't resist. We found secluded places all over the campgrounds. You could say I led him into temptation.

He was the one who insisted we get married. Our parents were freaking at first, but he was a religious Baptist and I was a minister's daughter, so they couldn't object to that. Our churches were different—you could say black and white—but when our parents met I think they were relieved to see how much Bible talk they had in common. We had a small wedding in my hometown, then he got into college here, and I got a job and started to support him.

Things got weird fast. We didn't know each other at all, and were very young—both just eighteen when we got married. He had a hard time in college, couldn't adjust, and finally dropped out when he was halfway through. He wanted us both to move back and live with his parents. I said no way, I was working, even if it was only cleaning jobs. The owner of one of the salons I cleaned, an older lady, she saw something in me and asked what I was gonna do with my life besides mop floors. I said I wanted to have my own business someday—a salon just like hers. I don't know why that popped out of my mouth. I'd never thought of it before, though I had had a little experience here and there doing hair relaxing, my grandma had taught me how to do cornrows, and I used to cut my little brothers' and sisters' hair every now and then. Mama said I had the touch.

This lady, the shop owner, said she would lend me the money to go to beauty school—interest free. I don't know why she wanted to help me, but I jumped at the chance and never looked back. It wasn't long before she offered me a chair in her shop, and I eventually paid back all the money I had borrowed. It took me nearly five years of working part-time to get it done,

156

but I did it. The minute I graduated I had work coming out of my ears. Everybody was standing in line to get cornrowed, braided, curled, relaxed, you name it. I'm still socking it away, and I'll have enough for my own place in a couple more years. Right now this suits me just fine.

My career never suited my husband, Ron, though. One difference between our religious families was that mine spurred me on to achieve goodness and excellence, and his seemed to cut the legs right out from under him. His parents practically disowned him when he flunked out of school. They'd have made our lives miserable if we went back there, so I told him, "Never, I'm staying put." Besides, I was getting my feet under me, and having a sense of what I could accomplish in my life. And I loved the people-aspect of my work. Talking trash all day with the other stylists and the customers, playing music, the shop owner lookin' out for us like a mother hen, always something to look at on the street—it was super lively.

Ron got all worried that I was mixing it up and having a good time, and he wasn't. What kept us going was that we still went to church together. He liked my church, and the sisters all made a fuss over him. One of the sisters there took us to the ice rink for the first time, and I loved it. After the first couple of times, Ron stopped going, and trips to the rink became my salvation. It's a bummer that Ron didn't get into it, but he never got into much of anything, just worked a few low-paying jobs here and there, and volunteered in charity work a lot—he was pretty good at that. He was always good to me, and I knew he loved me, and he still wanted to have sex. I think it was hard for him because he acted like it was still a sin, even though we were married. Looking back on it now, I'd say he had some kind of depression thing going on.

The night I met Carlton—my second husband—I knew immediately that he wanted me, and I liked that. I was married but that didn't matter. He came right up to me while I was skating, without the slightest hesitation. He said he had been watching me for a while—something I already knew. He was aggressive. I was immediately attracted to him. I like a man who knows what he wants and goes after it. It shows leadership skills. He didn't play games or give me some line. He said very honestly that he just wanted to skate with me, and even though he couldn't skate at all, I said okay.

Right away, I told him I was married to a white guy named Ron. Carlton gave me a look like he was judging me. Maybe he wasn't, but I've been accused of being an Oreo, so I figured it might be an issue. "Married?" he asked, raising an eyebrow. I shrugged, said "Yeah," and then did a few more laps around the rink by myself before going back up to him. "That doesn't necessarily mean I'm happily married," I said. I told him if I weren't married I would pay attention to him. Yeah, I was into him. He was cute.

Most guys hit, git, and then treat you like shit. I married Ron—my first husband—because he wasn't like that. He treated me nice. At first I thought I loved him; then I realized I didn't. I told myself I could learn to love him, but I never did. He cared for me and kept right on caring, long after my interest had worn out. That turned out to be a problem because when things finally ended, he turned the whole separation into a fatal-attraction thing. You know what I'm talking about . . . stalking me, turning up at my work, threatening me. Calling all the time. Sending deranged gifts. He turned into a real wack-job. The gals at the salon nicknamed him Velcro 'cause he was so sticky.

I was already off Ron—emotionally I mean—the night I met Carlton at the rink. At the end of the night, Carlton took my number and said he'd call me. I knew it was wrong since I was still hitched to Ron, but I didn't care.

A few weeks later I saw him again. We went out a few times and then we slept together. I got into bed with Carlton because I was in love with him. After that first time, we did it anywhere, everywhere, with no condoms or anything. I was so happy when I got pregnant. By this time I was ready to lose Ron, so I got pregnant on purpose by Carlton. Carlton said he'd always wanted to be a daddy.

Even though I was having another man's baby, Ron didn't want to divorce me. It didn't matter, though, because I was already gone, emotionally. I didn't love Ron. But Carlton, I did love—for a while. It took some time but finally I got a divorce from Ron and married Carlton. Ron went back home to his family. I wished him well but had the feeling that he was making a move in the wrong direction. Still, who am I to judge? It's all in God's hands, anyway.

At the time, I was still paying back my school loan, so I had very little money. Carlton made some money for a while doing construction until he lost his job. I was like, "It's okay, you can get another job." I thought we had a good relationship that we could build on and eventually we could also build up our money together. I knew I was going to have money no matter what happened because I'm a hard-working girl. I felt like we could grow together in a relationship and our finances would grow, too. I was wrong about all of that.

I went back to work full-time after our baby was born. Carlton got another construction job after we had our first child, but he lost that one, too. I helped him look for another kind of job but nothing was working out. I was starting to think he was weak and I was losing respect for him. I was the one working, making money, building my business, taking care of our daughter, organizing all her schooling and child care—he hung out with the guys from the neighborhood, doing shit. But our daughter was in kindergarten then and doing really well, and I had my friends from work and from church, so it wasn't totally bad. You gotta play the hand God deals you.

Then, I got pregnant a second time—this time it really was an accident. I was on the pill. That put me into a bad situation. I have to stand on my feet at work, and in my business if you ain't workin', you ain't makin' money. After a while, I just couldn't work anymore, because I was too pregnant. I really depended on Carlton to make some money, but he let me down.

That's when I realized I'd made a big mistake. It was my fault. I didn't know him before we got married. He was twenty-nine and I was twenty-five. He'd said he wanted to be a daddy, but he wasn't ready for a family. Turns out he didn't have any leadership skills. He didn't have faith in anything, not even in himself. He leaned on me like I was his mama, when I was supposed to be his partner. It was his mama's job to raise him like a man—not mine.

Over time, I lost my respect for Carlton. He was fired from four jobs on me and didn't work after that for a long time. I worked the whole time and then helped him get back on his feet. I only stayed because of our kids and because he needed a place to live. I feel like if you can go out and help a bum, why can't you help someone you know? Helping him also helped my children. They loved their daddy even though he was a loser. But I couldn't stand the sight of him.

He leaned on me like I was his mama, when I was supposed to be his partner.

He'd ask me to have sex, even beg me. To make the point that I really didn't want him, I'd strip down, lay on the bed, and open up my legs. I'd just lay there while he did his thing. It was like, get yours and get off. That let him know I really wasn't interested. When I first met him I was all into it; I was on top of him like a jackrabbit. I loved him a lot. I put my all into it back then, but by this time I was done.

That's when I started in with all the other men. Like the one I met at a little taco stand near my home. He was always there when I was, picking up food to go. One day I went up to him because I just felt like I wanted to have sex. I chatted him up. It turned out that he was forty, though he didn't look it, and at first I didn't like the idea of such an age difference, but a forty-year-old man sure knows how to find a G spot. He had a big old giant dildo, too, with all the different attachments that come with it. It was a machine. And it got me humming.

I didn't think of it as cheating. I was suffering because of

Carlton. I could have booted him to pursue my own happiness, but I felt sorry for him, so I let him stay. But I couldn't get into any serious new relationship while I was still married—men aren't interested in that. I was stuck . . . and it was all because of Carlton. He didn't have a thing left to give me. He lived in my house but I was an independent woman.

I can't even count how many men I've slept with since I've been married. At least twenty. I like doing it with different men. Right now I'm playing the field and I'm getting to know a lot of men. It's not just about sex. I want a relationship—but I do like sex. Might as well enjoy it while you still got it.

One guy who was totally into me chased me down at a party, and then he brought flowers to my salon. I thought he really liked me. I was looking for him to be a friend and have a real relationship with me, because my relationship with Carlton was dead even though he was living in my home. But that guy wasn't looking for anything. Just sex, that's it. He was great in bed, so I stuck with him for a while. He'd do things like tie me up and spread good-tasting stuff all over me and lick it off.

He was good, but most of them were. Men are nice . . . the way they move, the way they handle me. I like to be cared for. I like to be wanted. But there's more. I've learned something profound.

I came to figure out that I wasn't just playing around on Carlton as a booty call. I was getting back at men. I was looking for revenge. Some of the men in my family—even in my church—grabbed at me a lot when I was growing up. I think in some ways that has made me submissive on the outside and willing to just go with any man who seems to want me. But it made me furious on the inside, and that's also why I like to come on to men and try to manipulate them. It makes me feel like I'm in control of the situation.

Just a few weeks ago, I slept with a young guy named Dion—he was really great. His family owns the building where my salon is. He came inside one day to pick up the rent check. He was checking me out while talking with the owner. I just felt like I wanted to do a little something with him. "Can I have a piece of you?" I asked. Dion loved that I showed confidence and said he'd be happy to oblige. I told him that I'd be skating after work if he wanted to meet there, but he said he'd much rather have me come to his place when I was finished. He gave me the address and so I went to meet him around ten that night.

Dion and his father have this big old giant house. Dion answered the door. He offered me a beer and then we went straight up to his room. We talked and watched TV and then we got started fooling around. It was okay but he had his tongue in my ear while his hands were in my pants. He was all over me, but he wasn't very smooth. It wasn't like it was with the older guys who knew how to read my body.

He seemed to like me but he turned out to be a jerk; he didn't return my phone calls, and he was always busy when I asked for a little sugar. Now I've moved on to another young guy named Madison. He's twenty-two and he's working on his master's degree already. He's really cute—doesn't come right on to you. He's playing a little bit of hardball and I like that kind of challenge. I'm workin' this one.

Things are different for me than they used to be. The skate rink used to be off-limits, but now a lot of the guys I have sex with these days are from there. I've known some of them for a long time. There's a comfort zone there. They know I'm still married to Carlton, so they don't get serious. It's just sex with them. They love the sex; I love the sex. Doesn't seem like anyone's getting hurt.

We don't have a phone at home, so my guys call me on my cell phone. Since Carlton's finally back doing construction, I can spend the night with these other guys and I just tell him that I'm working. I style hair for videos and things like that, so I've been known to work overnight. I can tell Carlton I'm going over to my sister's house. Sometimes I am, sometimes I'm not. He never knows what I'm up to. With my men, I usually just stay for a couple of hours and then go home.

Time's my biggest problem—actually the lack of it. I ride the bus two hours to work and back, so that don't leave me a lot of time for men. But I've got a good hustle going that works for me while I'm in the salon. It's easier than getting a guy to come in for hair care. I see a guy I like and I tell him to come to the salon where I work so he can get a manicure. I tell him I'm struggling financially, I've got two kids, and I'm riding the bus to work. No mention of the husband, ever. Why should they help if they think you got a man at home? If I can get a guy to buy into my life, to come in and get a manicure to help support me, he's a candidate for a relationship and sex.

The other night I met a guy as I was walking down the street near the salon. He wanted to talk to me. He told me I was very pretty and asked if I worked in the area. I gave him one of my cards and told him to come in and get a pedicure and a manicure. I told him he looked like a man who's really into taking care of himself. He liked the idea of me stroking him up and down.

A week went by before he made an appointment. Then, when it was time to come in, he called back to try and break it so he could watch a basketball game. I made him feel really bad, so he ended up coming in, after all. We had so much fun. After the manicure, I massaged his hands while I asked him all kinds of questions—kind of like an interview. Just pay a little attention, that's all some of 'em want. Then he took me next door to Subway to eat. He paid, which I liked.

We ate and we talked and then he took me home. He was a really nice guy. He hasn't called me back yet. But I know he's interested, so I'm sure he will. That's how I'm working it now, bringing them into the salon instead of going out with them right away. It's much better for my financial situation this way. And the way it goes, I probably don't want a serious relationship with anyone right now. I'm starting to have a relationship with my kids. They're growing up and I'm having fun with that. My daughter keeps me company now. She's five. I want to give my kids attention and love right now. I don't want a man to take me away from them.

The kids don't know that I don't love their dad. I don't want them to know. It would damage them and they'd never accept it. At least not right now. Financially I want to be able to do a lot for them and if I separate from him that's going to cause more friction in my financial department. Carlton doesn't know how to think things out. And that's another thing that just makes me tired. I have to plan everything and think out everything and be the leader in everything.

But these other guys I've had—they've helped me to know what I want when I do get ready. I'm going to leave soon, as soon as my finances get set. And then I'll be able to do it right. Deep down, in my heart, I don't like doing other guys while I'm still married. I know from my religious upbringing that it's not right. But in my mind, I'm just married on paper. If there's not a bond between the both of you in your hearts and if you don't respect the person you're married to, then it's not a marriage, because you're not two people as one. You're separate. That's what I am. I'm married. But I'm separate.

12.

Lights, Camera, Action

The Story of Shelley Quinn

*P*eople glanced up as Shelley walked across the room, as if they'd seen this pretty young woman before—and perhaps they had, in upscale advertisements and in made-for-TV movies, where her sophisticated good looks and savvy intelligence had landed her several supporting roles. Medium-tall, with long, glossy brunette hair brushed back and held in a stylish clip, she exuded comfort and style with a dash of movie star thrown in. Garbed in low boots, leggings, and a cashmere sweatshirt under a long, leopard-print fleece coat, Shelley joked around with the waiter, who knew her from various auditions. The restaurant was a regular place for Hollywood up-and-comers to see and be seen, where they found work between acting gigs—as Shelley had done.

Shelley responded to a flyer I had distributed. She called and said that telling her story to someone other than a therapist

167

*would help her organize her thoughts so she could better under-
stand what had happened. As an actress she hoped to one day
draw upon this experience.*

*Despite her playful, glamour-girl appearance, Shelley was
strong-willed and focused, direct, articulate, and analytical.
Expressing herself honestly was important to her. Throughout
our conversation, it was clear that work was integral to her life.*

'M WEIRD. I'm a loon. Half of me is traditional and conser-
vative—which is why I got married—but the other half is so
not like that. I'm wild and I do wild things. It's the actress in me.
And that's why I had an affair, two years after I was married.

My husband and I discussed early on in the marriage what
we would do if one of us ever cheated on the other. I always said
that if he came to me and admitted he had been unfaithful and
that he still loved me, I would take him back. That's the way I
am. I'm able to compartmentalize events in such a way that I
would put our overall marriage above one mistake, even if I was
very hurt. I knew I could forgive him.

Ben was just the opposite. He had very strong feelings
about infidelity. I knew from the beginning that if I cheated on
him, our marriage would be over. An affair would permanently
damage what we had, and he would never take me back. I was
forewarned.

We met in a bar when I was twenty-two. I had just graduated from college and moved to New York, not really knowing anybody. He was playing keyboard with a band the first time I laid my eyes on him, and I said to myself, *Well, what about him? He's cute.*

Some mutual friends introduced us, but he couldn't have cared less about me. It definitely wasn't love at first sight.

A week later he called and said, "Hi. This is Ben."

I didn't recognize him at first. Then I realized who it was, and we made plans to get together.

Our first date was one of those weekend dates, where you go to the movies and dinner and then you end up spending the night together—sleeping close, but no sex—and the next morning, you go to brunch and then go home and change, and then go Rollerblading. It was phenomenal!

Ben was the best-smelling guy in the world. It's a chemical thing, like two animals drawn together. We slept together on the third or fourth date. I was incredibly attracted to him—and I still am. I loved to touch him and kiss him. But intercourse was always difficult. He was much better at the making-out part— the smooching, the rolling around on the couch, the touching. But when it came to sex, he got so excited he would just plow ahead, like he was all by himself. He would just thrust away, showing no concern for my pleasure. We never had perfect sex, the kind that transfers you into another dimension. It was satisfactory and, well, good—at times.

But we carried on, the way most new couples do, meeting for dinner after work, seeing movies on Saturday nights, sleeping in on Sunday mornings and reading the paper in bed.

Everything was going smoothly until our first big fight. It happened about five weeks after we first started dating. I don't even remember what it was about, but I know that he stormed out of my apartment and didn't call me for four days; I was pretty bummed out but I felt like I had to play by The Rules. You know, the old "hard to get" routine, which says that the next time he calls you have to act like you're busy, as if you don't care. So I did just that.

I said things like, "Oh that's fine. You know, I've been really busy. . . . I went away with this guy from my acting class. Oh, don't worry; he's just a friend."

I knew that would get his attention.

Not only did it get his attention—he was furious. We had another blowout fight over the phone and he told me I was a psycho. I was shocked by his anger and immaturity, so I decided it would be best if we went our separate ways.

First though, I agreed to meet him for coffee to see if we could work things out. I made the mistake of admitting my little "Rules" game to him, because I'm an actress and I'm very truthful. I should have just stuck to my story, but I'm stupid and I blabbed. He didn't understand why I sort of lied. He left the restaurant and walked one direction up the boulevard. I turned and walked the other direction. And that was that.

We ran into each other again, weeks later, at a party. I saw him across the room. My heart started beating wildly; he took me into the back and said, "I've missed you, and I've thought about you." He asked me to dance, which was charming in an old-fashioned way. He smelled so good! I loved the feel of his arms around me again. We started making out a little bit, and we ended up back at my place. Maybe it was because we missed each other so much, but he was much more attentive to my needs; it was like we were actually making love together. At the time, I thought, *Well, maybe all it takes is a little practice.* We got together again, and things sailed along smoothly for about a year and a half.

But then two things happened that changed our relationship. I made the decision to become a full-time actress. Before then, I had taken some classes, but I felt the time had come to pursue my career full-steam ahead and put everything else on hold. Unfortunately, at the same time I decided to do this, Ben's father became terminally ill.

I think Ben broke up with me because it was such a hard time. I didn't want to break up, but it was probably a good thing given the circumstances. He wanted to spend time with his father; I wanted to focus on my career. We stayed apart for a year and a half, but even while we were not together, we were still in love with each other, and we kept in touch. Actually, we slept together every month or so. I had several boyfriends during that time. They were mostly people I met through acting classes and through work. They were all fun and really into me—a couple of the guys I slept with back then are still good friends of mine today. But my true desire was always for Ben. He was the one who stirred my senses the most.

And then, finally, we decided to try again and never looked back.

I knew we had issues, but I loved him and I wanted to be married to him. Ben's a very possessive, jealous, controlling person, but I felt that if I could be very honest about who I was and what he could expect from me, our marriage would make sense. I believed we could make it work.

Before we got back together completely, the sex seemed to be improving. He was much more into figuring out what I wanted physically and he didn't seem to mind when I told him what to do, like, "Oh, that feels good," or "Do it like this." But when we officially became a couple again, the sex went completely downhill. He just went back to grinding away, not paying attention to me at all. He ignored all of my physical cues. If I tried to get him to go easy or change position, he just ignored me. If I tried to say anything, he'd go, "Shhh!" It was like he just wanted me to lie there and take it. Fortunately, I can have orgasms pretty easily by myself, so when he finished, I'd touch myself, thinking he'd like to watch me. But he wasn't interested. He'd just hop into the shower and I'd finish by myself. Not the greatest scenario.

But I told myself that the sex wasn't going to be amazing twenty years down the road, anyway—no matter who I married. I tried not to focus on sex; I was going on the potential of what our life could be.

Even though I was up-front about what I needed, he wasn't up-front or truthful at all—he pretended to be a different person than he really was. He pretended to be cool with the whole acting thing. He pretended to love that I was strong, outgoing, expressive, and passionate . . . but when it came right down to it, all those things about me drove him nuts.

Before we got married, we talked about children. Ben thought that two years down the road would be a good time to start a family. I was sort of okay with that, but even at the time,

I said, "That's a ballpark estimate for me. I can't possibly know how I'm going to feel two years from now."

In the back of my mind then, I felt a foreboding that it was not going to work out for us in the long term. But I decided it was worth a shot.

The first year of our marriage was wonderful; I was the happiest I've ever been. I loved being married. We lived in a fabulous apartment and we were very much in love. I spent most of my time getting our relationship back in order, planning the wedding, buying the apartment, decorating our new home, and doing all the work of making a home. I was also devoting more and more time to my acting career, and assumed that my life as an actress—rehearsals, good-looking costars, commuting from New York to LA—wouldn't bother him since it was all part of the package. He was supposed to support my career choice just as I supported him in his decisions. But he didn't.

In the beginning, I worked hard at our marriage. And I felt like I was very clear about what I could offer and who I was. But Ben was not happy. He was uncomfortable with the reality of my acting career, and he was still very jealous and possessive.

He would see me talking to somebody—anybody, a director, a techie, an actor—and he would grab my arm and say, "Who was that?" or "Did you just take his business card?" and get very upset.

I'm an Aquarian. I didn't take that kind of stuff too well—I didn't want him controlling me!

The career issue festered between us. Ben was ready to start a family and thought that I should be on his time schedule.

But that meant giving up on my dream and I wasn't ready to do that. I had two choices—stay in New York and play the part of devoted wife-mother, or take a few years to *seriously* pursue my acting career first. I had a feeling I would be great at the wife-mother role, someday. But I wasn't ready to play that part yet. I wanted to perform, take singing lessons, get out and dance, take more acting classes, and make the connections I knew I needed to advance.

We both agreed that I would go to Los Angeles, commute back and forth, investigate my options, and give my career a go for four months. So that's what I did.

Commuting was definitely not good for our sex life. It went from mediocre to bad. Many times, I was dry and I couldn't become aroused. It seemed that my brain was attracted to my husband but my vagina did not receive the signals.

> *It seemed that my brain was attracted*
> *to my husband but my vagina did not receive the signals.*

I still tried to communicate and asked Ben to try different things in bed, but he couldn't bear the least suggestion. He took it all as criticism, even the littlest thing, like "It feels so good when you rub me there." Things like that would send him into a total huff, and he would withdraw and give me the silent treatment. The situation was very frustrating, and I would get upset and cry. Then, of course, performance anxiety set in.

To make him feel better, I would say, "It's me, it's not you." Meanwhile, he didn't have any finesse; he didn't have a gentle touch; he was fumbling and klutzy; he was stubbly and rough. He just didn't get what it was that I needed. I yearned for that sexual connection with him, but he interpreted my desire as demands.

I felt so bad about the whole sex thing that, I swear, a little girl, a character, emerged and I started to talk to Ben in baby talk, begging for tenderness from him, but the baby talk turned Ben off even more. Sex became less frequent and more of a burden. He masturbated more, which shouldn't have bothered me, but it made me feel bad about myself—that I had forced him to resort to that consolation.

After two months of commuting, I realized that there was no way I could find out in only four months if my career was going to take off, but Ben insisted that I stick to the plan. He gave me an ultimatum: either I would land a film, or a television show, or I had to come home.

Of course, as the fourth month rolled around, I hadn't landed a job and I knew I wasn't ready to give it all up to be a stay-at-home mom. I told Ben as much, and it didn't go over well.

He accused me of reneging on our deal. He said it was not what we agreed to. He called me a liar and accused me of misleading him. This was when the light bulb went on in my head. I knew that the marriage was over. We could never be the people we wanted each other to be. That's why I had the affair. Way after, my therapist referred to it as an "exit affair," a way to end my marriage.

I met Jean Claude through a mutual friend at a bar in Los Angeles one night when we were all out partying. On the surface, he was everything I could possibly hope for from a long-term partner. He had every criterion on my personal preferences checklist: highly intelligent, good-looking, tall, extremely witty, ambitious, and able to talk circles around people. He was a New York City native from a high-society family, with loads of money, very Park Avenue. He oozed sophistication. His blue-blood, white-collar, country club background reminded me of my grandparents. But he also had a crazy, wild, fun side, and that appealed to me, too.

It was love at first sight, on both of our parts. Well, maybe lust at first sight would be more accurate. He came on very strong at first, but I stuck to my guns, thinking, *I am strong enough. I'm married. I won't do anything.*

He did not care at all that I was married. He said, "Fabulous! Your starter marriage; we'll have our fling and then you'll go back to your husband in New York."

At first, we only saw each other among friends, maybe three times. After one party, he invited me back to his house; we fooled around but didn't have sex, so I told myself, *Oh, that's okay. We just made out. I still haven't actually cheated yet.*

Stupid!

Ben knew something was weird almost right away. He could tell something was different by my voice. He didn't know there was somebody else, but he asked, "What the hell is going on with you?" I insisted that I had just been busy working, and it was nothing.

Jean Claude turned me on, both physically and psychologically, with his entire being. He was carefree, fun as hell, and we would laugh about everything. I had never met anyone like that—passionate, impetuous, determined.

My vagina was totally responsive to him, maybe because he was new and exciting. I had been having sex with the same person for seven years, and it was *bad* news by then. Married sex is all about the routine: he'd come, I'd come, and that would be that. With Jean Claude, it was a whole new world. He had finesse, he had the touch, and I was having multiple orgasms every time we were together.

Jean Claude understood the playfulness of seduction, and he was very open about it. One night, he took me to dinner and said, "We are going to order every aphrodisiac on the menu. Then we are going to see a sexy little movie. Then we will go for a nightcap. Then I'll take you home and ravish you and in the morning, we'll start all over again." He sexed everything up—it was all about the pleasure for him. Usually in the morning I was so worn out from all the playing that it was hard to get back into my routine! The whole time it was as if I had two lives. In one, I was in LA, enraptured with Jean Claude; in the other, I was back in New York playing the wife that Ben expected me to be. It was a disjointed time, but it was good while it lasted. And then I started to realize that my relationship with Jean Claude was a farce—he turned out to be one of those flames that burns hot and heavy and then fizzles out.

For starters, he had major addiction problems. He was a raging alcoholic and he also abused drugs. The actual physical sex quickly deteriorated because of all of the stuff he was on. It got so that he would stop in the middle of making love—literally, he'd be inside me—and pull out so he could snort a line or puff on a joint. He said it turned him on even more. It had the opposite effect on me. I'm no stranger to the wild life, but

177

I didn't want to be around drugs all the time. I'm eccentric in the other direction. I'd rather go to India and meditate, or something. Once Jean Claude's addiction was out in the open, he became hideous and very nasty—in and out of bed. It was clear that he didn't care about my feelings, my happiness, or my sexual pleasure. He just took care of himself. It was horrible.

I had been with Jean Claude for several months when Ben noticed our telephone bill and the long list of phone calls to Jean Claude's number. Even before Ben found the bill, I knew I needed to put the affair on hold, both for my sake and for his. I wanted to at least try to clear up things at home. I needed to sever the affair and end all communication, or there would be no chance to ever be with my husband again, especially if he found out I had lied.

When Ben confronted me about my strange behavior and the phone bill, I lied and told him Jean Claude was just a friend. I knew it was wrong to lie, but I did it to save my marriage. I don't know if he believed me but he let it go. We were both so fragile at that point. I ended the affair but, in a moment of weakness, wrote Jean Claude a letter saying that I missed him. I never sent the letter, but like a jackass, I didn't throw it away.

I decided to spend my thirtieth birthday in New York with Ben. It seemed like a good idea to do something to keep my mind off of the fact that my marriage was falling apart, so I planned a huge birthday bash. The party was intended to be a big show for our family and friends—to pretend that our marriage was great, when in truth, Ben and I were barely speaking—but it was a total and complete bust. Ben didn't give a shit that it was my birthday, and we ended up fighting over who would pay for the party. It was the unhappiest birthday I've ever had—what I remember of it. I drank myself into a stupor, trying to mask the pain I was feeling.

A week later, I begged Ben to go to couples therapy, but he refused. On Valentine's Day I gave him a gift, but he didn't open it. I said, "Aren't you going to unwrap your Valentine's gift?"

He said, "I don't want a Valentine. I want a divorce."

I said, "Fine. Fuck you. Let's file papers." It was very sad, but in hindsight it was inevitable. I flew back to LA two days after we filed. It was time to leave Ben and New York behind for a while.

As soon as I got to LA, I started dating.

Dating? That's a euphemism. I had seven or eight little flings, primarily sexual relationships that left me feeling even more alone and unhappy than I'd previously been.

Of course, I still saw Jean Claude from time to time. We would call each other at two in the morning to hook up. Our relationship dragged on for another year. I finally said to myself, *You are an idiot! Get this guy out of your life. He is toxic.* So I did, and we haven't spoken since. I don't miss him.

After I got rid of Jean Claude my personal life went down the toilet. I had no career. I was fucked.

I tried to keep myself busy with acting classes and part-time work that I got through a temp agency. I was going back to New York less and less often. At times, I would be very focused and healthy, going to the gym regularly and eating well. But then there were times when I'd go out on the town and the next thing I knew I'd be wasted, unhappy, bawling, weeping, and purging. My life was a combination of the good, the bad, and definitely the ugly.

The few times I had to go back to New York, I stayed at our apartment. Ben usually slept on the couch, but sometimes he would sleep in the bed with me, though we never had sex again. The strange thing is I wanted to have sex with him. Once the pressure to preserve the marriage was off, I felt even more attracted to him. I still loved his smell, and his familiarity. But all we ever did was hold each other and cry.

While I was packing the last of my things, Ben found the letter I had written to Jean Claude, and that's when he decided it had to end, once and for all. He told me I was a very bad person and he never wanted to talk to me again.

After that, things happened quickly. The divorce was finalized, we sold the apartment, and I packed my life into boxes and moved to LA for good. It was the lowest point of my life. I was a divorcée (yuck!), working in the restaurant industry to make money to pay the bills. I missed my New York friends, and my career was nonexistent.

About a year later, Ben called and said he was coming to Los Angeles and wanted to see me. He had been having a hard time dating other women; his job had ended, and he had been drinking a lot. He was exhausted from trying to avoid his pain. He thought that by looking into our lost relationship, he could answer some questions about future relationships and why he was having such a hard time.

I was cautiously optimistic.

It was really awkward at first, because we didn't know what to say to each other. He told me over lunch that he had tried to go out, but that every woman he was with irritated him. He didn't know what he wanted and was worried that he would never get married again. Despite all we'd been through, I was attracted to him again. I found myself wanting to kiss him, to smell him, to hold him.

When he drove me home after lunch, I invited him in. I had been arranging old photo albums, so we started looking through them and the memories, good and bad, came flooding back. It was very difficult for both of us.

We had lunch again the next day, and that lunch was a little less awkward. We joked and laughed about the good times, and I realized how much I'd missed him. I decided that if he came back and said he could accept me for who I was, and could accept my unconventional lifestyle, I would take him back immediately.

I started to drop hints about him moving to LA. But the conflict was still there. We rehashed all the same things we'd been over so many times before—my need to work, his desire to start a family. He wanted a timetable that he could hold me to, but I couldn't give him one. He still had bad feelings about my cheating; he said we had different attitudes about trust, fidelity, and basic moral values. The truth is that I had betrayed him and he had trouble getting past it. He wanted children right away; I didn't. As much as I wanted to get back together with Ben, I knew it would never work. He would never be supportive of my career; he'd always be suspicious.

When we finally said goodbye for good, I threw myself into my work, stopped drinking, and started paying more attention to my emotional and physical health. It paid off—my career is finally on track. I've got plenty of work, and I'm developing in ways that I couldn't have easily done if I'd stayed with Ben. My affair with Jean Claude was not the best choice, but it pried me out of a marriage that wasn't right for me.

13.

Brave New World

The Story of Ourite Raphael

*M*eeting Ourite Raphael was a lucky coincidence. My husband, Mark, had invited me to tag along on a business trip, booking us into a five-star hotel with all the amenities. The night we got there, he was needed at a business dinner with his boss, so he surprised me by scheduling a massage. That evening, I slipped into a luxurious white robe and waited in the "quiet room," a glass of cucumber-citrus water in hand. An olive-skinned beauty with thick, long, wavy jet-black hair and dark eyes called for me. "I'm Ourite. I'll be doing your massage today," she said in an Israeli accent.

Lying naked on the table, it suddenly occurred to me that in her line of work, Ourite might have some interesting stories to tell. I told her about the interviews I was conducting in hopes that she'd refer me to a few new women. "I've had an affair or two myself," she said. "You could interview me." I invited her to *join me the following morning for breakfast while my husband was meeting with a client. Ourite said she'd love to, as long as it was away from the hotel. After agreeing to meet at 8:30 at a nearby café, I allowed myself to relax under her strong hands.*

Although Ourite supported herself by giving pleasure to others through massage, she hadn't found any pleasure in her marriage. She was one tough cookie, I learned, having served two years in the Israeli army before relocating to the United States. Despite the hardships she had endured, and the strength she exuded, she admitted to crumbling in the presence of her domineering mother. Their stormy relationship launched Ourite's twin journeys—from Israel to America, and from ingénue to vamp.

*T*HERE'S AN expression we have in Hebrew that refers to a place you don't want to go to or a corner you don't want to touch. That's how I thought of my bedroom when I was married to Glen. I hated it that much.

Glen and I met at my parents' house when I was on furlough from the army. He was the American cousin of a neighbor. Our marriage was encouraged—you could say arranged—by both sides. He was an American living abroad, and he was planning to return to the States. My mother had always wanted me to have a better life in America, and after a suicide bombing at a local pizzeria, she grew desperate. She thought that my marrying Glen would be my one-way ticket out of Israel. She also assumed that Glen had some money and could support me. After all, wasn't America the wealthiest nation in the world? Naturally, if I married Glen, she and my father would follow us to America.

My army service started right after I graduated from high school. I was a virgin, completely inexperienced sexually. I'd had boys for friends, but had never dated anyone, partly because of the hassle I knew my mother would give me over whoever I brought home. Glen arrived in Israel while I was away with the army. My parents pinned their hopes on him as soon as they met him, and subsequently worked hard to cultivate a relationship with him. They were forever inviting him for Shabbat dinner, where they would tell him stories about their beautiful daughter who would make such a wonderful wife.

When Glen and I finally met, I thought he was okay. He wasn't bad looking, and he liked me enough. It would be an adventure, a connection to the States. We never officially got engaged—Glen didn't get down on his knee and propose or anything—but within a few weeks of our meeting, my parents and his cousins were talking about our wedding and planning it as if it was a fait accompli. I went along with it because it was impossible to stand up to my mother—even though something inside me was already resisting. Right before my wedding, I asked this good-looking guy named Itai who was in the army with me to take me to bed. "I need to have sex with you," I said. "I want to have some experience before I get married."

Itai looked surprised, then laughed, and said, "You're going to have the time of your life!" We went to his house one weekend when everyone was away. His room was clean and spare, with white walls and a pale carpet. There was a futon on the floor and a vase of scented lilies by the bed. The futon was covered with army blankets—"To make you feel at home," he joked. His humor relaxed me immediately. It felt good to be with Itai. We had already been through a lot together. When you're in the army, you learn to rely on each other for survival. I smiled and moved toward his strong, familiar body. I knew I could trust him to take me where I needed to go. I thought I could separate lust from love. That was a big mistake. My experience with Itai was incredibly passionate. We laughed, enjoying each other, and he took his time and let me explore him, inch by inch, leading me slowly through arousal to completion—and my first orgasm with a man. He was very gentle and skillful. That afternoon was sheer delight for me, and would become the yardstick against which I would measure the performance of all of my future partners.

I thought I could separate lust from love.
That was a big mistake.

As I went through all the planning and preparations for my marriage to Glen, I was still captivated by my experience with Itai. I thought I was in love with him. Of course, looking back, it now seems as if I was in love with the idea of being in love—but I have never forgotten the passion we shared.

My parents hosted the wedding in their backyard. It was a pretty low-key affair with just family and a few close friends. My mother beamed as only a Jewish mother does. Shortly after, we packed our bags and headed for the United States of America, with my family in tow.

Glen and I were on shaky ground from the day we stood under the *chupa*. The first year we were married was okay, but I had already decided that I didn't love him. Our sex life reflected that from the beginning. I always wanted more from him—sensual passion, more creativity in bed. He could never give me that; it just wasn't in him. He wanted me to love him and baby him. Sexually, he was shy and inexperienced. He was unsure of himself. I spilled the beans and told him I'd had one affair, when I was in the army. It was bad enough that I, as a woman, knew how to clean and shoot an Uzi—even worse that I was sexually experienced. He was a virgin when we got married, and he was very devout. I think he was anxious that I might be comparing him to someone else—and I was.

I convinced myself that I needed to stay with him, but during our marriage I had flirtations, and a few sexual experiences—once with a couple, although I liked the girl more than I liked the guy. One night when we all went out dancing, this woman, Lisa, and I fell for each other the way kids do. You know, like when you're seven years old and meet someone you just love, and you want to hold hands and sit close and snuggle with them all the time. With us, there was an immediate sexual component as well. After the evening of dancing, she invited me over a couple of times and we giggled and smooched and played with makeup—just like little girls! We put the music on loud and ended up dancing right into her bed. I guess you'd say we had a fling, she and I. Later, she said it turned her husband on to think of her with other girls. I never bothered to ask Glen how he felt about it.

Technically, I was married, but I didn't feel married because, isn't marriage supposed to be about love? I didn't have any regrets about what I was doing.

We had one additional problem. My mother had been wrong when she assumed that Glen had money. His salary as a book-keeper wasn't high enough to let us put any money away. His family was what Americans call "middle class," so they couldn't help us. With no money to play with, it was frustrating to think of all the things we couldn't do.

After three years of boredom at home, and little affairs here and there, I left for the first time, and moved back in with my family. Every Friday at our Shabbat dinner, my mother would look at me like I was a failure, and would bring the family into a conversation that was always the same:

"What were you thinking?" my mother would ask.

Then from my father, "How can you find a better guy from dis one?"

And my bubbe would always chime in, "Who is going to take you?"

Finally, I couldn't stand the pressure anymore. Glen, with my parents' encouragement, came to get me and I went back with him. He had lost so much weight, he looked horrible. His sad puppy face made me feel like I was taking someone's life. Guilt. There was so much guilt. So I stayed.

Inside, I asked myself, *What am I doing?*

I would tell myself, *I have to try again.* And I did try to want him the way a woman is supposed to want her husband.

But my body never followed along. He never aroused me; I was dry, and we had to use lubricants just to do it. It was weird— strange and unsatisfying. Glen was hesitant and unsure of himself, because he was unsure of me. He knew there was no love in my touch. I was pretty selfish, not thinking about pleasing him or caring about what he liked, not bothering to show him what I liked. We never had good sex and were totally unconnected emotionally.

I never even had a French kiss with him—we never even kissed on the lips. That should have been a sign to me from the beginning. A French kiss is all about passion and simple pleasure. I didn't have it with him.

When he wanted me to get pregnant, I pretended to be excited by the prospect of becoming a mother. The truth is, throughout our marriage, I was taking the pill. I had no desire for him; I was constantly drawn to other men. Wherever I looked, there always seemed to be somebody else I was more attracted to.

My sisters would tell me about their wild sex lives, and I would tell them about how I fell asleep after watching television by myself until four o'clock in the morning. Once in a while, Glen and I would sit on the couch and talk about life and art and music. He was very smart and funny, but nothing to do with the bedroom part of our lives was working for me; it just wasn't there. Sex was physically painful; I was always tight, and I didn't even feel sexy with myself. I felt like I was doing it with my brother. He was always polite, concerned, and anxious. I think he felt guilty about enjoying himself, even though he was desperate for me to be happy and wanted me to respond to him in ways I never could. During sex I would look at the ceiling or at my watch, praying he would hurry up and come. Even though he was asking for sex all the time, pleading like a little puppy, he left me cold. His touch was always tentative, questioning. He would look at me, and I would always have my eyes shut. Not giving him what he needed made him want it more. When we weren't having sex, he was masturbating. I saw him do it so many times; I even encouraged him. I said, "This isn't bad. You can do it."

We stayed together for about five more years, but I was lying to him the whole time. I had another tiny affair, and I was flirting with guys all the time, going to bars and acting like a single woman. I didn't like to have intercourse with these men, but I fooled around, doing everything except the dirty deed. I would make out with them in their cars, in my car. We'd use our fingers, our hands, and give each other orgasms, and that would be it. Once or twice I even got this guy off standing up against the building in the dark lane behind the club. It was a kick, an adventure—sexual experimentation, but it still felt as if everything was missing in my life.

I hardly ever saw Glen. I was waking in the morning, going to work, having my flirtations at night, going dancing, going to clubs; I would come back home at midnight or 2:00 A.M., and he didn't even ask me where I'd been because he was scared of hearing it. He didn't want to let me go. He never knew how to say the right things at the right time, so he decided to keep quiet and not talk about things. That was one of the biggest issues between us; we swept everything under the carpet instead of dealing with it. In a way, it was also comfortable for me that way. I could do whatever I wanted. Nothing would change.

Meanwhile, we hadn't had sex for months.

Then I met Mike. He was gorgeous. I remember thinking about a quote from a John le Carré novel—he said, "Come to bed, my little baby, and let Mummy teach you some of life's long words." Who knew I would end up with Mike? He was the concierge at the hotel where I worked as a masseuse. At the time, my job was my escape. I loved the tranquil environment of the spa, and I enjoyed going to work every day. Once my flirtation with Mike began, I hated to leave work at the end of the day. I counted the hours until I could go back. He would bring bottled water to my massage room every morning, and we'd laugh together and gossip about our coworkers. It was the best time of my life.

When I started falling for Mike, life was totally crazy. I developed a friendship with an older woman at the hotel who turned out to be in love with me. She totally spoiled me, bringing me treats and little presents, and inviting me for drinks or to dinner. It seemed like she wanted a sexual relationship with me, but she was about fifty or sixty and could barely walk, so I didn't think much about it. Then one day she hit on me when we were alone in the massage room. She just grabbed my crotch as if I was a man. It had been a mistake to lead her on. Letting her down gently wasn't easy.

Meanwhile, Mike and I were getting closer. Things really heated up when Mike walked into my massage room and locked the door. He turned to me without saying a word, grabbed me, and pushed me up against the wall. That kiss was long and hard and so incredibly sensual. We tumbled onto the massage table and had the most incredible sex. It was so intense, like a crazy moment, and it made me feel like I was free again. As if I had never left the army or suffered through a boring, lifeless marriage. Every day after that we would share a special moment in the privacy of the spa, on my padded table, in and out of the hot tub or the shower. He didn't know I was married, and I didn't exactly tell him right away.

Mike and I began spending more time together. He invited me to his home to drink a coffee and listen to music. I still hadn't told him that I was married, because in my mind, I wasn't really married—I didn't love Glen. It didn't matter to me that we lived in the same house, because he wasn't in my heart. Still, at that point I probably should have set the record straight. But I didn't. When we were together at his home, away from work, I felt every vein and all of my blood come alive. I missed the feeling that I had in the beginning, with my first lover, Itai, the guy from the army. When you are a teenager and you fall in love, you feel that every emotion, every feeling you have is saying something important to you. You know exactly what you want and how you want to do it. It's not only about sex; it's about communication. It's about how you see life—with someone else, through them. I never felt that way with my husband.

Mike awoke those feelings once again when he came into my life, but when it slipped out that I was married, he got very angry and said he didn't want to have sex with me anymore. He screamed, "Infidelity," and emphatically said he couldn't go there ever again.

His brother had been the victim of an adulterous wife; while he was away in the army, his first wife had cheated on him with her boss. This was all too familiar for him. For several weeks he refused to have sex with me.

I said, "I don't want to bother you with anything serious. I just want to have sex, for God's sake! It's been a long time since I've had anything and I need to!"

Mike said it was important to him to know that he was not a rebound. He is a super-sensitive guy—not a typical man. I told him that I could show him better than I could tell him what he meant to me.

By the end of those two weeks—when he was refusing to have sex with me—I was in love. Crazy in love, and I didn't want to hurt him. There was something about this guy—he had these really big baby-blue eyes and when he looked at me, my heart would just break for him.

I give myself credit as a woman for coaxing him into my bed. My butt is pretty good; I work out every day to keep in shape, but I think it was my persuasive argument that we could do it without hurting anyone that convinced him. Finally I wore him down and he said, "Okay! Enough! Let's do it! No expectations!" He later told me that he was always horny for me.

We went to his house. He was big on electronics and had music in every room of the house. There were huge speakers under the bed. The sound throbbed while we were making love. It was like the echo of our hearts beating together. He sang to me—it was sweet and funny—and massaged me all over as well as I could have done. Then he asked me if I was ready to make love, and that was it! It was like dancing a sexy, hot dance, with the best partner I ever imagined. Two weeks later I said, "I'm moving in."

During those two weeks before I decided to move in with Mike, I went back and forth between the two houses, Mike's and my husband's. I told Glen that I was going to see a friend, that I was going to see a movie, go grocery shopping, get my nails done, or this or that. I couldn't even keep track of the lies, because there were so many. Eventually it took so much energy to hide it that I just got lazy about the whole thing. I was bursting inside. And it was weird, but my husband still didn't know.

Each time I'd come home from being with Mike I'd see Glen's pathetic face, that puppy face, and it said to me, "Have mercy!"

But I was tired of having mercy. I just said, "Fuck it." I didn't care.

I realized I couldn't stay with Glen anymore and just have sex with Mike on the side. I wanted a full relationship, total involvement. It was too hard to have sex with Mike, put on my clothes, go home, and leave it all behind—I loved him and felt like I was betraying him. When I did it a couple of times, I felt like shit. And it was always hard waking up next to Glen when all I wanted was to wake up with Mike.

Chemistry is the only way to describe what Mike and I had. It was a pure and simple chemical reaction between us. A good affair and intense sex life is totally about smell. I loved Mike's smell. I loved his skin. Never in my life did I think that I could give a guy a blowjob and enjoy it like ice cream. He tasted like vanilla to me. I wanted to eat him. I never in my life went down on guys before, even in my flings. It was something I couldn't do with just any guy; it was way too intimate. I needed to have something special to create this kind of desire for a man.

If you asked my husband, he would tell you that I was the worst partner in bed. If you asked Mike, he would tell you that I was the bomb! I was the best thing that ever happened to him. With Mike, every inch of his skin looked, felt, tasted, and, especially, smelled delicious. I was addicted to him. I could touch him for hours. I don't think it's because it was the beginning of the relationship, because it's been like that since we met. It was never like that with my husband.

It was difficult for me to leave my husband at first. I was the main support, and I felt that I owed him. I continued to pay his bills, his health insurance, car, and all that stuff even while I had the relationship going with Mike. I continued to deposit my checks in our joint account, because I felt bad for running out on him. Technically, I had an affair; but to me, it wasn't an affair because my emotions were done, and we didn't have sex for a long time before I even decided to have the affair. I had been sleeping on the couch for months. Finally I said, "I can't give him more than that. That's it."

For me, life began when I took my pillow out of the bedroom and moved it—and my heart—in with Mike. My relationship with Mike had started as an affair, a break from the misery of my marriage. I hadn't thought about where it would lead, only that it was a great escape route.

Once I finally left Glen, I was very clear in my conscience, especially because I gave him a lot of money; you could say I bought my way out. Usually it happens the opposite way, with the man buying the woman out. But I felt good that I had taken care of all his debts and his schooling, and that I paid the rent and all the bills and everything, even when I wasn't there.

Glen told me in the end—before we got divorced—he said, "You know what? I knew all along that one day I would not be good enough for you." I didn't tell him he was right, that I never thought he was right for me.

In the beginning, I didn't tell him that I had moved out to be with my lover. Instead I said that my housemate, Mike, was gay. One day not long after I moved out, Glen and I had to do a bank errand together. We went to lunch afterward, and it felt very weird. It was nice to be with him in a different environment, with no expectations of anything except lunch. When I looked at him, I couldn't understand how I'd spent so many years with him.

He was trying to leave the door open so that we could get back together some day. At one point, I told him I wanted to try, because I didn't want to make it permanent for him or even for myself, in a way. But every time he called, or I called him, I could feel his pain over the phone. It was time to end the charade.

I did a one-eighty in my personality after only two months of living with Mike. I went from not wanting kids at all—because I didn't want to raise children with Glen—to feeling desperate for a baby with Mike. I'm sure I probably scared him with all my talk about kids. He was getting cranky—almost going crazy, but I stayed pushy. Somehow, I convinced him to marry me.

Mike is actually very much like Glen in a lot of ways: kind, good, loyal, sensitive, what you see is what you get. There is no bullshit. It's different though, because with Glen I felt like I was his mother. I controlled the money. I controlled this and I controlled that.

Even though I make more money than Mike, I feel equal to him. I'm very empowered and demanding in my work, but when I go home to him I get to be a little girl; a little wife; his woman. He isn't able to provide any financial security. In fact, the guy doesn't have a pot to piss in, but boy, he's sure got something to piss with!

Even though Mike and Glen have many qualities that are alike, they are very different in the way they communicate. Aside from the horrible sexual frustration in my marriage, my ex brought out other bad qualities in me—especially in the way I dealt with problems. He made me nasty; I didn't want to cope with anything. Sometimes he would look at me, and I didn't care that he was frustrated. He didn't even know how to say what he meant or to ask for what he really needed. After a while, I didn't care what he wanted to say or what he needed. When he would try to hug me, I used to laugh, like, "Why are you hugging me?"

When I have a fight with Mike and I'm giving him the silent treatment, he demands that I talk to him. I learned from Glen that the silent treatment worked great when I didn't want to deal with problems, or with him. But it never helped anything.

With Mike, I'm a better wife; I'm a better woman. I'm cleaning my house—I never cleaned my house. I let my husband do all that shit before—I never did the laundry, never did shopping, never; and now I want to do everything. I want to create a home for him. A place for us to make love and grow our love. I'm very protective of this love, and I want to take care of it. In a beautiful home, a clean, alluring place.

I was miserable for many years but didn't know what I was missing until I hooked up with Mike. You know that you have a bad relationship—that you have bad sex. You just think that what you have is the best you can get because you are afraid to find better.

But I found better. I didn't know what make-up sex was until I met Mike. I'm telling you, it's fun. It's crazy! You get so cranky when you're feeling like shit, you argue, and you are at odds, then both of you go to the same bed anyway at the end of the night, and suddenly every touch that he's putting on you has so much meaning, and you are full of love all over again.

My mother was so angry with me when I left Glen for Mike. It occurred to me that I had gone along with my mom's plan to get married to satisfy her. When I disappointed her she became meaner than you could imagine. She stayed mad for a very long time because I left my husband—twice. I had spent too many years trying to make everyone else happy except for myself.

You can't please everyone.

I blame my mother for pushing the marriage on me. I blame myself for taking so long to figure out that Glen wasn't right for me. Call it a sixth sense or something, but I knew in my stomach, back in Israel, that it wouldn't work. There were too many issues from the start.

Today, at thirty-one, I can explain what went wrong. Glen never raised his voice. I always knew when I opened the door that he would smile, be there, and always stay loyal, with no big surprises. He was good for me, for a while anyway, because he calmed me down and stopped me from going and fucking around with every guy. But once I met Mike, it was all over.

My affair with Mike was the best decision I've ever made. I have a very short life story, but it ends happily. At first, I felt guilty, but now I am having wild sex instead of awful sex—or no sex at all. It has been a healing process, almost, like finally finding myself. I'm sorry that it had to come at Glen's expense, but I live with the hope that he will find another woman to make him happy. He deserves to have a woman feel about him the way I do about Mike.

14.

The Spice of Life

The Story of Anna Leung

*A*nna had a zest for love and life unlike that of any woman I'd ever met. She was from a large and lively Chinese-American family, with a strong work ethic and a reverence for education. She had a multitude of positive role models from her parents and her many aunts and uncles. Her cousins and her siblings were high achievers in business, the learned professions, and the arts. Her family milieu was very competitive, but also loving, supportive, and good-humored.

Anna—a young-looking thirty—was petite and emphasized her facial features with her bangs cut straight across her brow. Her long hair sported a chic, angular cut. She was dressed for our meeting in slim slacks and a little jacket with eye-catching trim. She looked businesslike, with a dash of creativity, perfect for the high-tech field in which she worked. She spoke perfect English, but a faint Chinese ring emerged from

*time to time, becoming more pronounced when she got ani-
mated or when she parodied her family, which she often did.
Her ironic sense of her own foibles complemented her clear telling of her "wacky" story. And wacky it was.*

*Anna was the youngest in her family. She was brilliant,
motivated, and determined to keep up with her older siblings.
As a result, she skipped two grades in school, entered Stanford
at the age of sixteen, met a boy and got married at nineteen,
had her first baby at twenty—and her first extramarital affair
at twenty-one.*

∞

I MET KENT in college. He stood out—he was six foot three,
white as they come, with smooth, lean muscles. His features
were nondescript; he just looked like a nice guy from Minne-
sota. He wasn't traditionally attractive, but he wasn't unattractive, either. I liked him; my family liked him. He was smart and
had a lot of potential. Enough of my cousins had married non-
Chinese that it was no longer an issue. And he adored me—an
attractive quality in a man.

Having a boyfriend, being engaged, getting married—that
was all part of the family dynamic; that was what everyone did,
and a wedding was just another occasion to celebrate. Mine went
on for three days. We had a Chinese ceremony near my hometown, in the Buddhist temple. And in the days leading up to the

ceremony, we took over various restaurants and clubs for all the pre-wedding showers and dinners. Next, we moved the whole shebang up to the Ahwahnee Hotel in Yosemite for a Western-style wedding. Yee-ha, it was a lot of fun! The whole process was so over-the-top, the groom was almost irrelevant.

Kent was my starter marriage. I always knew that. I couldn't look him in the eye the day I married him. By that time I was already pregnant. For me, an abortion was out of the question—not that I'm against it, not at all; but I really wanted a baby, and so I just went through with the rest of it, the marriage and everything. That was just what we did. My family was always supportive; they rallied around the minute I told them I was pregnant. This was a normal part of life.

Sex had always been a point of contention between Kent and me. It was often a painful experience. Kent was very well endowed—huge!—but clumsy, and he often pushed right into me before I was really ready. He would have an orgasm immediately, within thirty seconds, so it was incredibly dissatisfying for me. I would crawl into bed each night, not wanting to touch him, thinking that sex was something I had to get through. He tried dealing with his problem. He even went to a doctor, but I had already reached the point where the sooner it was over, the better.

Meanwhile, I wasn't altogether unhappy. We had a beautiful home, we had this amazing daughter, Taylor, and I was doing really well in school. Everything was okay. I wasn't fulfilled, but most people at age twenty are still trying to figure out who they are. I thought I had it all—for the time being, anyway.

It wasn't like I didn't communicate. I dropped hints to Kent about my feelings for other men. When I met Terry, I said, "Wow, I met this great guy—he really likes me. He's an old guy, but he's so hot, blah, blah, blah." Maybe he thought I was just kidding around. He should have paid a little more attention. He always told me, "I love you, I love you. I'm afraid you'll leave me." But when he almost lost me to another man, he had nothing to say. He put his head in the sand. That was the problem with him—he had no spine.

Terry was my first affair. I met him when I was just starting my master's. I did part-time training work for a computer-consulting firm. He was one of our out-of-town clients. My attraction to him was instant, and magnetic. Total yin and yang. I remember the few days before we got involved. I was zapped by emotions I had never felt before. I'd never experienced an adult relationship where I was crazy with passion and aching to get physical with somebody. I was fascinated by my own response. When I met Terry, he was forty-eight. I told him I was twenty-eight, which was a lie, but it seemed old enough at the time. He never knew how young I really was.

The week after our introduction, there was a regional sales meeting and Terry came to town to oversee his staff. He specifically requested that I do his training segment, so I taught software classes to his employees all day long. I anxiously awaited every glimpse of him as he walked by or popped in to check on his people.

At the end of the day, he said, jokingly, "I want to give you your report card."

He folded up a piece of paper and handed it to me. It said,

"You are absolutely beautiful." I was blown away. I would have loved to spend some time with Terry that day, but I had classwork to attend to, and he had responsibilities to his staff. So we went our separate ways, but I couldn't stop thinking about him.

Terry was living in North Carolina with his wife, and I was in Palo Alto with my husband. After that trip, I would make love with Kent just so I could fantasize about being with Terry, which was crazy, because we didn't even know each other! I was shocked and excited when he called me a week later to say he was coming into town for a follow-up conference and that he wanted to see me.

We didn't waste any time. Our relationship started and ended in the bedroom. We had a great time for several days. It was a highly charged affair, equal parts emotion and sexual ecstasy, although I tend to think at that stage in an affair the two are synonymous.

Terry told me he wanted to leave his wife. I did not want him to dump his wife for me. That was way too much pressure, especially since our age difference was pretty big. It's not criminal, but it's bad to lie to seduce an older man. Terry thought there was a twenty-year age difference between us, instead of almost thirty, but it didn't seem to matter much to him. It mattered to me, though. I knew it was wrong. A forty-eight-year-old man should not sleep with a twenty-one-year-old woman; it's just not cool. Still, I slept with him as often as I could. During our affair, I kept up a physical relationship with my husband, just enough to keep him happy and unsuspecting. Quick and easy, that was Kent.

The way things turned out, my affair with Terry lasted about four months. We saw each other only three times during that period. Once more in Palo Alto, and twice in Chicago. We talked on the phone frequently. Those four months were among the most exciting times of my life. I was yearning for passion, for that sexual connection, and at the time, I wanted it to go on and on and on.

Each time we saw each other, he mentioned that he wanted to leave his wife, which became increasingly unsettling for me. I knew that while I loved him at forty-eight, I wasn't so sure I would love him at fifty-eight or sixty-eight. Then I began to think about what I was doing to the woman on the other end.

I tried to justify our affair by telling myself that if he wasn't sleeping with me he'd probably be sleeping with someone else. But accountability doesn't allow for hypothetical outsiders. I had become entangled in the affair, so it would be my actions—not those of a hypothetical third party—that knowingly destroyed two families.

Looking back, it's hard to understand how an almost fifty-year-old man could consider his twenty-year marriage disposable. How could he throw away a lifetime of memories? It's frightening.

When Terry told a friend that he wanted to leave his wife, he gave Terry great counsel, saying, "Get what you need out of this fling and then go back to your wife and kids."

His friend was right, and that's what Terry did. It was absolutely the right thing, but I can honestly say I have never felt such intense feelings of love and lust for anyone since Terry. When my daughter, at her young age, talks about really liking so-and-so from a school dance, I reminisce about early-life emotions and the intense desire that goes with them. These young feelings are powerful, as powerful as they are when you're a grown woman, but they usually don't lend themselves to good decisions. I still think about Terry in those moments.

Toward the end of our affair, my company had a billing problem with Terry's company, which created a chasm between us. Then, around that time, my mother died, quite unexpectedly. She was not much older than Terry. This really threw me; I was her baby. That time was the closest I have ever come to losing my mind. My family all huddled around me. Without them, I don't know what I would have done with my grief. My mother's death made me all the more cognizant of the precious gift of my own daughter. Meanwhile, Kent overheard me talking on my cell phone and figured out that I was involved with someone else. He confronted me repeatedly until I finally just confessed.

Terry's wife never found out about me, although she had been asking him if there was someone else. I wondered how she could believe his denials. Don't you just pick up on the change in your spouse? It seems impossible to sustain such a lie for longer than a few weeks. I told Terry that Kent knew about us and I needed some time. It was a relief. I stayed close to home, and healed, and played with my daughter. I tried to persuade myself that passion wasn't the most important thing. I also tried to rev things up at home with Kent. It didn't work.

I was twenty-two when my second affair happened. I was working on my doctorate. Franco was a post-doctoral fellow and my summer-school teaching assistant. He was twenty-six.

I was never one of those girls who fit in with her husband's friends. They all went to Metallica concerts and I thought that was weird. I related much better to the nerdy math and engineering crowd. I understood them and preferred the straightforward nature of smart, awkward people.

When I met Franco, there was instant "karma" between us. He had on these silly white socks made of Turkish cotton with no elastic in them—I remember focusing on little things like that. He always wore jeans and a white T-shirt; he had olive skin and black eyes, and he was already losing his hair. He spoke flawless English with an irresistible Italian accent. I found out from a secretary in the engineering department that he was considered the smartest man on campus—and I had his attention! He thought I was a little Asian hottie. I was sold the moment I laid eyes on him.

Because I was so attracted to him, everything I said to him had a spin. I wanted to be noticed. I was wildly attracted to his look, in the same way I'm attracted to Harrison Ford. I don't like pretty boys. He was teaching a class the following semester and everyone knew that he and his girlfriend had broken up. On campus, we intentionally ran into each other on a regular basis. We talked a lot, but we were not physical with each other.

Then I did a home pregnancy test and found out I was expecting. Kent and I were still having the same, boring sex—with our usual frequency, and my usual disappointment. Despite my intense interest in Franco, I was enthusiastic about becoming a mother again. It seemed to connect me with my own mother, whom I missed terribly. I was a great mother to

Taylor, and delighted to be pregnant again. But within weeks, I started to bleed, and I knew something was wrong. I miscarried soon thereafter.

Poor Kent—he had to deal with my sorrow. It wasn't his fault, but he couldn't do anything right. When I got irritated, I would lambaste him. I was looking for a fight. A miscarriage is painful and emotional, and even though the pregnancy was unplanned, I was distraught by the loss. Looking back, I shouldn't have been surprised that he was emotionally absent—I probably pushed him away—but at the time, I was enraged by his attitude.

Killer headaches landed me in the hospital right after the miscarriage. Demerol helped at first, but when I started to abuse it, I became disoriented and my feet grew numb. I started to panic, thinking I might be addicted. When I finally refused a shot, the nurse was furious. I couldn't take it anymore, so I ripped the IV out of my hand and took a cab to campus. I found Franco, burst into tears, and told him about my miscarriage.

Franco held me for a little while and then suggested we get some lunch together in a nearby café. Perhaps it was because I was still woozy from the drugs, or because of the trauma of losing a baby, but I was smitten with him, enthralled by every little thing he did. I must have been desperately searching for a diversion. Anything to keep me from facing my pain. Demerol didn't help with the emotional aches. But Franco did—he seemed so exotic to me, even when he ordered food. I told him that I wanted a separation from Kent—something I hadn't even told Kent. I made Kent's presence in my life seem less intrusive than it really was. I lied in order to give Franco an opening—to see if he would jump. I was testing the waters.

What was I thinking? I had a child and responsibilities. Kent was not abusive—he was a decent guy, and he made a good living. He was kind and loving to our daughter. Many women want a sweet, kind man, and Kent was that. But apparently, that wasn't enough for me. I found him boring.

I tossed the ball into Franco's court to see what he'd do. We ended up driving across town so that he could show me where he lived. Two days later, he drove me there again. This time, he invited me inside.

When we got to his apartment, he lit a cigarette. I hated smoking, but surprisingly his hand-rolled smokes turned me on. I was mesmerized by everything about him: his brilliance, his achievements, his accent, even his smoking. He was so exotic to me, so different from the familiarity of my life. The catch was that I was too embarrassed to take off my clothes in front of him because I had stretch marks on my breasts from nursing for a year. I was not the hot little Asian thing he had been flirting with all summer. I was a woman with a history and it was written all over my body.

He was so exotic to me,
so different from the familiarity of my life.

I wanted to come back in the evening when the lights could be out. I told him I was wounded by motherhood, and he was completely beautiful about it. He loved my body so much that I soon forgot whatever issues were bothering me.

We were on the couch, making out, and I reached for the waistband of his boxers. He said, "Don't do that unless you're serious." Well, at that moment, I wanted him. I had to have him and there was no turning back. We went into the bedroom—the sex was incredible. He was an animal and we spent many hours in bed.

We were together for about a week until one night, when we were making out in his car, he asked me to move in with him. I said okay.

Then I told Kent.

I moved my daughter and myself out of our house the next week. Kent was devastated, but he didn't resist, or even protest. He helped me pack and then carried my things out to my car. It was so, so sad. He was heartbroken but believed that we'd get back together. His vision was always of us, and I didn't have the heart to tell him I would never be back.

I lied to him about Franco, said we were just friends, that we weren't having sex, that I just needed time to get my head together. I tried not to hurt him too badly, telling him anything other than the truth, which was that I was repelled by the thought of being his wife and sleeping with him. I was having wonderful sex with another man; but instead of being honest, I said I was going to get my own apartment. That was just one of countless lies I told.

We had been married for just over two years. I told my family and my friends that what I had with Franco was exactly what you wait for and dream of your entire life. I loved Franco more than I ever thought possible. It was much greater and more real than my love for Terry, because there wasn't anything to hide. Terry didn't even know who I was—it was a fictitious, fantasy relationship. With Franco, it was real. He was the right age, he was in the right social mix, he was good in bed, and I was mesmerized by the notion of a man becoming a professor.

I drove straight over to Franco's apartment and never left. We were married the following June. Kent didn't get over it for a long time, and has not remarried. He was always waiting for me to come back. Finally, he hooked up with another woman who seems to be psychotic. Despite everything that happened, he and I remained on good terms.

Life with Franco was great, but complex. He became a wonderful stepfather to Taylor. Children are never easy, but he loved her. I didn't realize it at the time, but the reason Italian men are so good with children is because they share so many of the same characteristics. Unlike American men, Franco was quite comfortable with Taylor's temper tantrums—probably because he had so many himself. He could have taught my daughter a thing or two about getting her way. Franco still didn't have a faculty position lined up, so he was in the midst of an identity crisis, which made him way more volatile than I thought he was when we first moved in together. At that point, he had the upper hand. I was the one with the issues—a failed marriage, a child, a devastating sense of loss. But I was willing to face my problems and try to restore my sense of wholeness. Franco, on the other hand, wouldn't open himself up to any kind of self-analysis.

I was interested in a fifty-fifty relationship of teamwork and friendship—like it was in my family—but it didn't work out that way. Our relationship became plagued with conflict.

Another problem was that I am not very good with money. I was always spending next month's paycheck. It was a point of contention. In Italy, there's no such thing as a credit card; you buy when you have the cash to pay.

Franco and I fought a lot in ways that I have never fought with anyone. There was a lot of physicality. He couldn't handle rejection, so if I tried to get away from him he would stand—literally—in my way. Then I'd push him and he would push back. We would hurt each other. It was like being on a playground except there wasn't a supervisor to step in and break things up. This went on for several years and spiraled downward into black eyes, broken furniture, even arrests. It was a conundrum: Despite his being an intellectual and basically a decent person, he was culturally wired to think violence was okay as long as there was a lot of love, too.

My cultural background was radically different. I was used to a more reserved, indirect way of fighting. Plus, I was the baby and used to getting away with things. Whenever Franco and I had a fight, Kent would pick me up and take me out for coffee. He saw Taylor regularly, too. He was a good father to her, despite the split. And he was always there for me. Until I discovered I was pregnant. That's when he realized I had lied to him about my relationship with Franco, that we were more than just friends.

I was twenty-five and had finally gotten my doctorate. I wanted to find a good position, even though I was pregnant with my second child. But when Franco was hired to work on the super shuttle, we packed our bags and headed for Florida. It was a huge sacrifice for me—leaving my home, my roots, my family, and going to what I thought of as a redneck frontier—but Franco hadn't been able to find a teaching position and this was an excellent opportunity that could open a lot of doors for him.

Once Franco was settled into his job, he didn't like the way the project was set up so he refused to play by their rules, and got fired. His family stepped in to help us out, which had its ups and downs. Franco was considered the black sheep in his family because he was so gifted intellectually. He was an Italian nerd. An interesting combination.

Sometimes Franco's relatives would come for a visit and not leave. Franco's family was loud, animated, and fun-loving, but they kind of took over the household. The decibel level would increase exponentially with each new arrival. Sometimes I would think they were all arguing, only to run in and see they were laughing. In Italian you can't tell the difference. They talked all the time. Two of them would bump into each other in the hallway and they'd still be yakking it up two hours later.

Suddenly, I was in a position where I couldn't say anything about what went on in my own home. How do you say "privacy" in Italian? There's no translation. How perfect is that?

In fact, it felt like hell. Franco and I had way too many fights. And we shed more blood than we ever should have. The police came to my house time and time again, but I still didn't want a divorce. Despite the violence, sex with Franco was always passionate. Instigator or not, I was enticed into bed with him, year after year, and always satisfied.

Eventually I started to crave unconditional love and started a flirtatious relationship with a former classmate after I give birth to my second daughter. It was the perfect antidote to the tension at home. For some reason we never had sex, although I would have liked to. Franco did not reach his potential in Florida, but I did. With my Ph.D. in hand, and strong faculty recommendations, I was offered an assistant professorship at Brown. We left his crazy family behind and moved to Providence. Franco didn't really want to go, but he realized that I was the one whose career was starting to thrive. During my second semester at Brown, I was invited to a conference at Yale. It was there I met Philippe.

Philippe was Swiss, thirty-five, funny, and divorced. He made me laugh all the time. I love to laugh, and I loved joking around with him. I was long overdue for some good humor by then. I was certain that we would sleep together very soon after. I was way off on that one. We did get physical—he kissed me one night after a meeting. But when I let him know that I was up for more, he pulled away from me, saying that people should be married before they have intercourse.

I choked, flabbergasted that any man would feel that way. I insisted we go to a movie, because I wasn't going to let him get me all aroused and then pull away and say we couldn't have sex. It wasn't natural—he'd been exploring my body willingly for hours and yet was refusing to have intercourse. But refuse me, he did!

Maybe it was a Swiss thing. Once, in a restaurant in Geneva, I ordered a ham and cheese omelet but the waitress wouldn't let me have it. She pointed to the menu, which read, "ham or cheese." I couldn't have both. Maybe they were like that about other things, too.

I didn't see much point in rearranging my life to be with him when he was closed off to the idea of sex. So we chatted online night after night and then engaged in what I now know is called an Internet affair. The Internet is a funny thing. You can be flirtatious and push the boundary of what's acceptable without even being in the same state. We had e-mail sex—which apparently isn't a sin in Switzerland—and shared a lot of laughs. For many months, this helped fill the gap I felt at home with Franco. There wasn't much laughter around our house.

Finally I told Philippe that if we couldn't be together, I would have to end things. Reluctantly he agreed to meet me one night at a hotel. The anticipation was foreplay and the sex was epic. I was head over heels in love with him immediately. Marital life was not what I had expected it to be like, but I had to stay with Franco because I was a lowly assistant professor with two children in private schools. And I had other financial obligations to maintain. It was hard work making a good life for my kids, but that's all I ever wanted . . . for my kids to have everything. The dynamics of my marriage changed drastically once I took over paying the mortgage. After I became a professor, I wouldn't let Franco talk down to me anymore or make me feel bad. Everything he had hanging over me evaporated. I didn't need him anymore, so the balance in our relationship changed, leaving me wondering if I still wanted him. He never cheated, wasted money, or lacked integrity. And he was pathologically loyal. Still, that wasn't enough for me. I knew that things would not last between us.

One time when I went to meet Philippe, Franco broke into my computer and read several intimate, sexually explicit e-mails from Philippe. He screamed, "You lied! You betrayed me. I never did anything like that to you." He was right, but what he did do to me—the bruises and scars—was something I didn't want to live with any longer. I felt like one of the Yanomamo Indians from Brazil, where the woman with the most scars on her head is considered to be most loved by her husband.

Despite the passion between us, the years of abuse eroded my respect for Franco. Philippe gave me pleasure without the drama or histrionics, so he won. We've been married for eight years, and the pleasure is still there, and deepening. They say the third time's the charm. I don't think I'll be tempted to cheat again, though you might want to check back with me on that one. History has a way of repeating itself.

15.

For Love or Money

The Story of Nora Reilly

I met Nora several years ago at a women's spa up north. I was visiting a girlfriend, hoping that the change of scenery would unclog my mind. Nora had taken the same exercise class as I and was in the sauna afterward, by herself. While the other women chatted amiably with each other, Nora held herself aloof. Casual bonding with strangers was clearly not part of her agenda.

She spoke to me only because I was glancing through a prestigious financial magazine. She said, "I'm in that issue," and told me her name. There with her picture was an article she'd written on risk management. I noted that she was associated with a big brokerage firm, and I asked her about it. She made it clear that her job was merely a steppingstone—she had plotted a trajectory that would take her well beyond her present position. When she asked what I did, I told her I was *a writer. Her interest dissolved as soon as I said it, though she asked perfunctorily what I was working on. When I told her about this book, she nodded and closed her eyes. The conversation was over. After a while, she got up and left, without another word.*

I noticed she wasn't in the exercise room the next day, but I didn't give her another thought until a few days later when I was checking out. The receptionist handed me a small envelope containing a beautiful monogrammed business card with a scribbled note from Nora that said "Call me."

When I called, she was very brisk and matter-of-fact. She told me, "You have to do this project. And you have to hear my story."

She arranged a flight for me the next day and sent a limo to meet me at the airport. I was driven to an upscale Italian restaurant-bar that oozed understated elegance, just like Nora.

Nora was a tall, thin blond with shoulder-length glossy hair, worn straight and blunt. Dressed in a severely cut suit with a crisp white shirt, her look was provocatively expensive. She had on fine leather accessories, tasteful platinum jewelry, and exquisite high-heeled shoes that showed off her long legs. As Nora told me her story, it became clear that her dissatisfaction with her marriage, and her selection of a lover, were largely based on net worth. In Nora's world, sex was part of the display of one's capital value—something you used to leverage your way up the ladder. So, unlike the other women I had talked to, Nora's experience seemed to be much less about the pleasures of sex than about the allure of a powerful man—and the privileges associated with his stature.

Nora had tremendous poise, and she conducted herself in the manner of someone who is accustomed to being looked at. Throughout our conversation she kept her voice low and even, her calm demeanor punctuated occasionally by a toss of her shimmering ice-blond hair.

∞

I HAVE TWO lives. In one life, I am a successful stockbroker, married to my handsome husband of twenty years. I am a responsible parent with four happy, well-rounded kids. In the other life, I am a free spirit, unhampered, and involved in an obsessive relationship with my current boyfriend. I live in constant fear that my two lives will collide and everything will blow up in my face. If that ever happens, I will be utterly alone.

For a long time I cheated on my husband with all sorts of men. I habitually worked late and I traveled a lot for my work. I made a lot of money, so it was easy for me to call the shots. I picked up new lovers as easily as I picked up new accounts. Plenty of men were willing to play my game. I told some of them I was married, and I let others believe I was the carefree, wild, single girl that I pretended to be. It was easy, because nothing ever got too serious. If an affair became anything more than a fling, then I just cut loose and moved on to the next.

Sometimes I didn't even bother to call it an affair. I indulged in a little quickie here and there. Sometimes I kept it short—one time and that was it. But with others I preferred to linger—for weeks or months, until it played itself out.

My most memorable fling was short and sweet. I was coming back from a meeting in Seattle. One of the other participants—an older man, tall, attractive, extremely wealthy, and well known in corporate circles—was particularly intriguing. We had lunch together, and there was no doubt we were attracted to each other. After lunch he offered me a ride to the airport. Cozying up to me in the back of the limo, he looked me right in the eye and said, "I don't usually go out of my way, but I'd like to fly you home in my jet—or anywhere else you'd like to go."

I didn't say yes or no—I just leaned over and kissed him, hard, on the mouth. I was ready to join the mile-high club.

There was no one onboard except him, me, and the pilot. He popped open a bottle of champagne and we sipped, smiling at each other. I undid my top button and he took it from there. He said, "I want to appreciate you like a rare treasure that I may never find again." And he did! It was exhilarating—no strings, no promises, just the two of us, above the clouds. Hours later, we landed, our appetites sated. We parted warmly, and never saw each other again.

That wasn't the first time I sampled a man just because I liked the looks of him. I love intrigue and power, even if they only last a short time. It's a thrill.

I don't know why I became this way. I like to think it was because my husband, Steven, didn't measure up to my standards. When we met, he was about to take over his family's real-estate business, and he had visions of expanding in the high-end market. He was young, good-looking, and had the family name behind him. Over the next few years, he overleveraged his properties. When the market crashed, he took heavy losses and went deeply into debt. Now he's managing mostly down-market holdings. He's not a slumlord, exactly, but only a rung or two on the ladder above one. Anyway, he isn't too happy about the image he is now projecting.

> *That wasn't the first time I sampled a man just because I liked the looks of him.*

I was disappointed, even upset, that he didn't become as wealthy and successful as I thought he would, and that I had to become the major breadwinner. Maybe I started cheating because I thought I had been cheated out of a lifestyle I deserved. Maybe it's because I believed there was something better out there, and I never stopped looking for possibilities. Maybe it's because I met so many men through work—there are certain personality types who are inevitably involved in the risk-trading world of business and finance. Maybe the affairs made it possible to keep up my relationship with Steven—sometimes it was nice to go home and sleep with him again, after a fling. Maybe I simply enjoyed the risk.

I first met Ryan at a friend's birthday gathering, in a posh restaurant reserved exclusively for the party. We noticed each other right away, and I must admit that I was impressed with his reputation as an enormously successful restaurateur. I also knew he was married—and it was well known that he did more than flirt with women outside of his marriage. We flirted a little bit that night, and even though I got the impression that he would gladly have taken things further, I was already in the midst of another affair and had no intention of starting anything new.

After that, Ryan was definitely on my radar. We had several acquaintances in common, and we often ran into each other at one event or another—art openings, charity events, private parties. I even set him up with some of my friends, but nothing ever worked out. As time went on, we became more and more friendly, and although nothing actually happened between us for some time, we managed to hang out together, often using our kids as an excuse. I arrange a lot of my kids' social lives— they are still pretty young, three, five, seven, and ten. Ryan and I would get our kids together for play dates at the park, for movies, or for dinners now and then. Totally innocent, of course.

Then there was the pivotal moment. One night, Ryan and I decided to meet for drinks. He selected a very posh hotel with a quiet bar, where we could sit unseen. We spent the evening becoming comfortable in each other's presence. We smiled and laughed and fooled around under the table. At some point, someone walked by and said, "You two should get a room." I looked at Ryan, wondering if he would move on that idea. Then out of the blue, he said, "Do you think you could fall in love with someone like me?"

I was shocked. This was too crazy for me.

"I've got to go," I said unconvincingly. "It's ten at night and I've got to get back to the kids."

"I can get us a room," he said.

"Maybe another time," I said.

He didn't call me for a week.

When he finally did call, he suggested we meet for dinner. I wasn't sure what he was thinking—whether he was punishing me for blowing him off, or whether he'd just been too busy to call. He had a way of being both stoic and abrupt all the time. I didn't feel that I knew him well enough to press him on his feelings. But there was something unsettled, a tension between us that we didn't address.

Over the next few weeks, it got so that we were fooling around every time we saw each other—kissing, touching, caressing—and then finally we slept together. One night, in a quiet corner of an upscale bistro, he said, "If I weren't married, I'd be coming at you like a freight train." He started kissing my neck, slowly, and running his hands over my thighs—not at all like a freight train, but with the lightest, teasing touch. I knew I had to respond. I said to him, "I don't know what you're doing, or who you're seeing, but I'm not seeing anybody else. If we're going to have any kind of physical relationship, I don't feel comfortable if you're sleeping with somebody else." Meanwhile, both of us were married to other people—but that wasn't even an issue.

"I'm not seeing anyone else," he said. At the time, I believed him. Had I known how many others there really were, I might have stopped the affair right then. Or maybe not. The truth is, I thrived on being with Ryan, who, as busy as he was, knew how to make those moments of pleasure seem important, and made sure that every detail of our trysts was perfect. He treated the affair like an event, with money no object and every detail planned—just the way I thought things ought to be. Good champagne and 600-thread-count sheets were always part of the picture. He set the scene as if he anticipated all of my desires. He seemed to know what I expected; he was in the league to which I belonged. I always acted unimpressed by his efforts. During foreplay, I tried not to react—not even to breathe—even though I was aching to respond. This drove him wild. Finally, when we were both almost in a frenzy, I let myself go—and we would both have these amazing, earth-shaking orgasms. I was drawn to his passion and persistence. Our sex was really different from sex with anyone else I'd been with. I kept him intrigued by remaining distant.

I didn't mind at first when he'd get on his cell phone and resume work as soon as our lovemaking was over. His cell phone rang constantly, and he was always running off to take care of "work." But as the relationship progressed, he lied to me about where he was going, and I knew that he was still going out with other women. His habits, his manner, and our whole connection were all very deceitful—I'm including myself in that description since we were having an illicit affair—but I couldn't stop seeing him; the allure was too great. Then one weekend he disappeared. When he finally called, it was pretty obvious he was with somebody else. I later confronted him about it; I couldn't take it anymore. He tried to apologize but I was strong and stayed away, for a while at least.

Eventually I got sucked back in. He kept calling and calling. One day he sent a car to pick me up and take me to a hotel where he met me in the bar, full of apologies and desire. Of course, I stayed for a drink, then dinner; then we went upstairs, to the penthouse. The room was full of fresh white flowers, and the champagne was already on ice. He really knew the drill. I knew he had other girlfriends, but I didn't attack him for it. I didn't want to appear too demanding and scare him away.

During that same period, Steven was getting a little suspicious, so I started spending more time at home, devoting a little more time to him. I paid extra attention to things that I usually wouldn't bother with—things like our finances. I also made a point of initiating sex more often. We actually had more sexually gratifying moments around that time than usual. I was probably working off the energy that I would have spent on Ryan. With my husband, anything I wanted to try in bed was fine. I could get aggressive and act out on him all of the things I restrained myself from doing with Ryan. I can't say I didn't enjoy the look on Steven's face—that is, when I wasn't fantasizing that he was Ryan with my eyes shut tight.

My husband didn't seem to have a clue what was going on. I had to go to Detroit for a business trip, and Ryan was supposed to come with me. He canceled at the last minute because he was throwing a party for some bigwig at his restaurant. He had the nerve to tell me it was strictly for business, but I wasn't stupid. I went on the trip and conducted my business, and when he called, I let on that I was happy and that all sorts of men were pursuing me. It seemed to work like a charm, because there he was at the airport right when I stepped off the plane. He said he was miserable at the thought of losing me.

Even though Ryan's not the most attractive guy, he knows how to use his charm to attract women wherever he goes. It's instinctive, like a reflex with him; and he never stops. When he pulls up in his Ferrari, women fall all over him. He's got something magnetic, even beyond his obvious success and his enjoyment of it. He has intelligence, a sense of dominance and worldliness. He's a competitor, a true alpha male—with a sensitive, intuitive side that makes him care about what people think of him. These are the things that attracted me to him in the first place.

The sex is also fantastic—it's passionate and wonderful every time. We usually get two hours of lovemaking every day. His penthouse is our *pied-à-terre*. I leave some of my things there, and sometimes stay and work after he leaves. But I do wonder if we can keep it up—if everything would be as good if we were married or if we lived together. It's not as if he's coming home at night and I'm doing his socks. He's not living with me. He doesn't see my nagging side. I know I'm not the easiest person to get along with. I'm grouchy and moody. I know if he saw that part of my personality, he'd be pretty disillusioned. So for now I'm just enjoying the excitement and the drama.

Still, I need to believe there is something more than just sex between us. But I'm not naive. I know I can't expect a full committed relationship from Ryan as long as we are both married.

Ryan and I have come a long way in our relationship. I trust him more now than I ever have. There was a long time when he probably thought every woman was fair game, but I don't think he's fooling around anymore. Now, I know he really loves me. He tells me all the time. It took him a long time to say it, but now he says it, and I think he means it. He even actually got divorced along the way—not necessarily because of me; but it's still been a very good thing for our relationship.

Strangely enough, I still live my life as if I were a single person. Maybe I shouldn't have ever gotten married, but it's too late now. I have children, which is why I stay. I think kids would always rather see their parents together.

Steven eventually found out about us because I got careless. I charged a few pricey things for Ryan on my American Express card. Steven called to see what the charges were and put two and two together. Now Ryan is afraid of what Steven might do, but I don't think Steven will do anything, for a while anyway. Even though Steven and I have watched our marriage dissolve, he's never brought up the possibility of separation or divorce, and neither have I. We mostly keep it together by faking it, and this has worked for us so far. Nevertheless, I know that Steven despises me. He thinks I'm selfish and despicable. I don't care anymore. We're only together because of our four children. We have nothing to say to each other. It's sad, because we had always been close in a friendly sort of way.

Despite all of this, Steven stays with me. He knows I would never leave him, so perhaps he stays out of spite. More likely he stays for the kids, or because I'm supporting us all—who knows? I'm still afraid to push my luck. I never mention Ryan, and he never asks. What if Ryan leaves me after everything I've gone through? We aren't married, nor does he owe me anything. He could just vanish one day and never see me again. At least I'd still have my marriage, however much of a shell it may seem.

I also stay in this marriage because of the money. Our finances are complicated. We also have joint properties, which I would like to keep for the kids—I bought them, but they are community property. There's no way he could buy me out. I earn much more than he does, so I would actually end up having to pay him alimony. Obviously, neither of us ever says "I love you" anymore. Still, he's a good father, and the rest of my family thinks the world of him.

I don't think the kids have been affected. They have no idea that anything is wrong. We never spent a lot of time together around the kids, so nothing seems awry. With four kids, everyone is always going in different directions. I've always gotten up early in the morning, and Steven has always slept late, so our schedules never coincided, even from the beginning. We've always been separate beings with separate lives. I've always been the working, traveling member of the family. Everyone got used to the idea of our different lifestyles a long time ago.

Still, I feel terrible having to lie to everyone all the time. Parents of my kids' friends have been pulling away from me—they seem to be friendlier with Steven. All his friends and relatives hate me. They all tell him to divorce me and get on with his life. I am beginning to feel shunned.

Even Ryan's family knows my whole story, and they think I'm no good. His brother and sister have made it clear that they're appalled that he's going out with a married woman. They're always judging us. It's so humiliating. Every night I'm torn in two, or three, or four. But I also know if I were just with Steven and had nothing else to look forward to, I'd be completely depressed. I'm damned either way.

So I have these two lives. You would think that at least one of them would be idyllic, but instead they are both fraught with uncertainty and despair. If I had just chosen one and worked at it, then maybe it could have been perfect. I am too weak to choose one over the other, and besides, it's too late. Everyone sees me as damaged goods. It keeps me always on edge, always paranoid that people are watching me and judging me.

I tell myself that without pain there can be no pleasure.

I know I really have no right to complain about anything, because I've created this situation. I can still make the choice to commit myself to one of these lives and be done with the crazy dual existence. Nevertheless, I tell myself that without pain there can be no pleasure. And I wouldn't be doing this if I didn't get any pleasure out of it. But deep down inside I know the real reason I won't let go of either relationship: I'm afraid that I will fall. At least with two relationships, I have a bigger safety net.

16.

My Story

Part Two

*Y*ou now know how everyone's story plays out but mine. I owe you that.

The day of the trip to Sacramento finally arrived. Nick came to our house before Mark left for work. From the upstairs bathroom where I was getting ready, I heard Mark answer the door. "Just a second. I'll get Diane," he said, in a sticky sweet voice. He only sounded that way when he was trying to control some other, less flattering emotion. This was not going to be a comfortable morning.

Mark came upstairs into the bathroom and said simply, "Sweetheart, your date's here."

"It isn't like that, honey," I protested, capping my lip-gloss. "He's going to see his girlfriend, remember?"

"I'm sure of that," Mark shot back. "I'm just wondering who his girlfriend is."

"Aren't you okay with this trip?" I asked, hoping he wouldn't answer.

Mark put his fingers together and, as he loved to do, flashed me the sign of the "W." Whatever. . . .

I must have been nuts to think that Mark would let me go on the trip without making me feel guilty about it, but I was determined to spend the weekend with Nick, so I just blew him off. Grabbing my purse, I headed downstairs. Nick was standing in the entryway, smiling confidently. "Ready?" he asked.

I kissed Mark goodbye and called out to Mallory. "Time to go, sweetie."

Mallory came running out of her room, Barbie doll in one hand, bag of candy in the other. "Bye Daddy," she said. "I love you."

"I love you too, sweetheart," Mark said, without looking at me. "Have a great trip."

Mark and Nick carried the suitcases to the car. The dresser, my "reason" for taking this road trip, was already loaded. Pulling out of the driveway felt like a typical family trip, only uncomfortably different. "Bye honey. I'll call you tonight," I said, knowing full well that if the tables were turned, I'd expect three or four calls from the road. Mark said nothing, then turned back to the house.

Near the freeway entrance, Nick pulled into a gas station.

Watching him as he worked the pump and checked under the hood, wiping the dipstick with a paper towel, I wondered how he made this mundane task seem so enchanting. Was this love?

As we drove, Mallory chattered away in the back seat while Nick and I listened to music and talked about movies and books. I enjoyed the close comfort of our conversation.

Two hours into the drive, Mallory was fast asleep.

"Do you have dinner plans tonight?" Nick asked.

"We'll probably just eat at my sister's."

"Maybe we could have a drink together after."

"Aren't you going to be with Susan?" I asked, feeling a little jealous.

"Nah . . . she's only free during the day."

"You're driving all the way up here and she can't make time to see you?"

Nick hesitated before spilling the beans. "She's . . . well, she's married."

My stomach flip-flopped. *What was going on here?* I sat quiet for a few minutes, absorbing the news.

"How long have you been . . . together?" I finally asked.

"On and off for about twelve years." He could have been talking about the weather, his tone was so matter-of-fact.

"Does she have kids?"

"Five. She's in a blended marriage."

Suddenly it occurred to me that I really knew nothing about Nick. What would possess a single man to engage in a decade-long affair with a woman who wasn't available?

We drove along in silence for a while. I was trying to reconcile my feelings about Nick's being with Susan with my own feelings of desire. In the rearview mirror I could see Mallory sleeping like an angel in the back seat . . . my "protection."

"How about that drink?" he asked. "Think you can make it?"

"Maybe," I said. Just then, Mallory woke up.

The trip had flown by, and I realized that I only had another hour with Nick in the car. Not wanting our intimacy to end, I suggested we get lunch. At a roadside diner, we ordered burgers and fries, and then Mallory begged for some quarters to play "the claw." Nick reached into his pocket and produced a handful of change. He slid four quarters over to her. "Thanks!" she exclaimed, her face lighting up. Before our food came, Mallory had come back four times for more money. She was trying to catch a stuffed bear to give to Dewey as a chew toy. Victory eluded her but Nick's $5 bought us a chunk of alone time.

When we arrived—after dropping Nick at the hotel—my sister greeted me with a warm hug. Her kids were delighted to see their long-lost cousin, and they couldn't wait to get in the pool. Watching them swim, I wondered how I would explain Nick to Meryl.

The visit with my sibling was great. Meryl had gone all out for dinner . . . arugula salad, scallop risotto, ciabatta bread, and char-donnay. When had she learned to cook like this? As siblings, we think we know each other so well, but then everyone grows up, and your lives start to diverge. If she only knew what I was up to. . . .

We finished the dishes and then I told Meryl I was going to have a quick drink with Nick to thank him. "Maybe we'll catch a movie or something."

My sister didn't hide her disapproval.

I met Nick in his hotel bar. He stood up to meet me, looking elegant in a dark suit. He took my face in his hands and kissed me. He smelled divine. "I was hoping you'd come," he said.

We sat down, and he leaned over the table and traced my hand with his finger. I was dizzy with the newfound feeling of freedom. And desire. No one knew us, and I was so caught up in wanting him that I no longer worried that we might not know each other. His relationship with Susan and the spotty details surrounding it no longer mattered. The only thing that mattered was our mutual longing. . . .

Two martinis later we were headed for his room. Once inside, he pulled me toward him, moaning like a teenager. After months of self-restraint, I fell into his arms, ready to let loose. I was so attracted to him.

And then my pager went off.

It was my sister's number. I snapped back to reality and jumped for the phone. "Mallory woke up crying from a nightmare. She's okay but it might help if she hears your voice."

There was my little daughter, on the other side of town, and where was I? I looked around the hotel room. It was bland, nondescript, devoid of warmth or familiarity. I looked at the neatly made bed, then at Nick, his face flushed, his eyes expectant.

"I have to go," I said, rushing out the door. "I'm sorry."

The drive home was uneventful. After that, I avoided Nick's calls and e-mails for weeks, losing myself in the daily demands of family life. But I was still thinking about him.

Nick was persistent, sending me little notes and asking to see me, although I didn't respond. Instead of talking to him, I talked about him, to all the women I interviewed. My opening up to other women made them feel comfortable opening up to me. Hearing their stories was incredibly cathartic and way cheaper than therapy.

I told Mark about my trip with Nick, except the part that took place in his hotel room. Then I told him that I wanted to do this book. Mark took it all in stride. But he advised me to be brutally honest about my own story or the book wouldn't be authentic. I finally admitted to Mark that my feelings for Nick were deeper than friendship. Mark said he'd always known.

It took a long time for me to realize just how damaging my relationship with Nick was to my marriage. Mark was deeply hurt, but because I wasn't paying attention, I had no idea.

I'd like to believe that I would have acted responsibly had my pager not gone off that night, that I would have stopped myself because cheating on Mark would have been wrong for me. But who knows? Staying faithful isn't easy, especially when my desire to escape is constant. I'm attracted to good guys and bad boys—the only common denominator is their ability to help me forget my problems for a minute, or an hour.

Many of the women I spoke with had demons of their own. Others said their affairs were nothing more than marital enhancements. I've come to believe that "marital enhancements" *are* also escapism—if only from the monotony of marriage.

Ultimately, this book is a love story.

I also now believe that an affair can destroy a marriage or make it stronger. For women who are struggling with temptation, I hope this collection of stories provides support and guidance. It certainly did that for me. Peeking behind the curtain of their infidelities, I recognized myself in some of these women—particularly my pattern of running from my problems—and in so doing, I healed my marriage. I'm still a desperate housewife, but now I'm desperate to show my husband how much he means to me. Ultimately, this book is a love story, about finding my way back to Mark.